NOVA
BOOK O
Everything

Everything you wanted to know about
Nova Scotia and were going to ask anyway

John MacIntyre ▪ Martha Walls

MACINTYRE PURCELL PUBLISHING INC.

MacIntyre Purcell Publishing Inc.
232 Lincoln St., Suite D
PO Box 1142
Lunenburg, Nova Scotia
B0J 2C0
(902) 640-3350
www.bookofeverything.com
info@bookofeverything.com

Cover photo courtesy of Nova Scotia Department of Tourism, Culture and Heritage.
Photos: Pages: 8, 9, 32, 54, 66, 78, 96, 154 Nova Scotia Department of Tourism, Culture and Heritage.
Photos: Pages: 166 Istockphoto

Printed and bound in Canada.

Library and Archives Canada Cataloguing in Publication
MacIntyre, John,
Walls, Martha,
Nova Scotia Book of Everything / John MacIntyre, Martha Walls.
ISBN 978-0-9784784-3-8
1. Nova Scotia--Miscellanea. I. II. Title.
FC2311.M335 2005 971.6

Introduction

No book can be a book about everything, of course. Not even the venerable *Encyclopedia Britannica* can make that boast. What we've tried to do with the *Nova Scotia Book of Everything* is give you information that you should know; information that you might like to know; and lastly, information that is downright fun.

From the best-kept secrets, to five of the scariest criminals, to the best beaches, it is all here. We tell you how much we earn, how much we drink, and how many of us live rural versus urban. When we started this project, we had one guiding principle and that was to deliver a book that would be interesting, entertaining and useful.

The rule of thumb was that if it was interesting to us, it makes it in; if it doesn't, well, it sits on the sidelines. The problem we ran into was that time and space meant that there was plenty of stuff we would have liked to have included, but simply couldn't. Next time.

This is the third edition for this book and it has become the best-selling title in the province in the last five years. With this new edition, we have updated all available stats, added a new culture chapter, web links for further info, and a feature we know you will get a charge out of called "You Know You Are From Nova Scotia When."

Putting together a book of this type inevitably is a product of a team of people. Kelly Inglis served as master editor and director. Ian Gormley participated in a significant amount of the writing and research of the material, as did Wynne Jordan, Holly Gordon and Nick Hatt. Then there are the people who supplied us with the things they love, find peculiar, or just find downright interesting about Nova Scotia. They took time out of busy schedules, and we think you'll be glad they did.

At any rate, we had a lot of fun putting this book together. We hope you have as much fun reading it.

John MacIntyre and Martha Walls, 2008.

Table of Contents

Farewell To Nova Scotia

"Farewell to Nova Scotia" is the unofficial anthem for the province. It is a sailor's lament of unknown authorship. It is believed to have been written during or just before the First World War and is thought to have been derived from "The Soldier's Adieu" attributed to Scottish poet, Robert Tannahill. It was discovered by celebrated Nova Scotian folklorist Helen Creighton.

The sun was setting in the west,
The birds were singing on every tree.
All nature seemed inclined for to rest
But still there was no rest for me.

Chorus
Farewell to Nova Scotia, you sea-bound coast,
Let your mountains dark and dreary be.
For when I am far away on the briny ocean tossed
Will you ever heave a sigh and a wish for me?

I grieve to leave my native land,
I grieve to leave my comrades all.
And my parents whom I held so dear
And the bonnie, bonnie lassie that I do adore.

The drums they do beat and the wars do alarm,
The captain calls, we must obey.
So farewell, farewell to Nova Scotia's charms
For it's early in the morning I am far, far away.

I have three brothers and they are at rest,
Their arms are folded on their breast.
But a poor simple sailor just like me
Must be tossed and driven on the dark blue sea.

Nova Scotia:

A Timeline

10,000 Before Present: An estimated 12,000 to 75,000 Mi'kmaq live in Mi'kma'ki, their territory consisting of the eastern half of the Gaspé, New Brunswick, Prince Edward Island, Newfoundland, mainland Nova Scotia and Cape Breton Island.

1497: Giovanni Cobatto (John Cabot) lands on Nova Scotia, and whets European appetites with tales of the massive cod stocks of the North American coast.

1524: The term "Acadie" is first used by an Italian explorer Giovanni da Verrazano, to designate a large region of northeastern North America.

1605: First French Settlement is established in Nova Scotia at Port Royal, near present day Annapolis Royal.

1606: The first social club in North America is established; the Order of Good Cheer, which encourages regular merriment and feasting, is established to help settlers at Port Royal pass cold, lean, winter months.

1610: Mi'kmaq Grand Chief Membertou is baptized by Jesuit missionaries, becoming the first Catholic convert in Nova Scotia.

1613-1763: Nova Scotia is a North American battleground in a series of wars and skirmishes between France, England and the Mi'kmaq.

1632: Three hundred French settlers, the first "Acadians," establish a thriving French colony in Nova Scotia.

1713: France establishes Fortress of Louisbourg, a truly multi-cultural fortified community on the edge of the continent, at Cape Breton.

1749: Halifax established by Britain to counter French Louisbourg.

1752: North America's first newspaper, the *Halifax Gazette*, is established.

1755: Eleven thousand Acadians (about 75 percent of all Acadians) are expelled, sent around the globe by Britain, when Acadian loyalty comes into question after 300 Acadians are found defending the French Fort Beauséjour. Acadians refuse to take an unqualified oath of allegiance to Britain.

1758: Fortress Louisbourg falls for the second and final time to England, marking the beginning of British rule in Nova Scotia.

1740s-1750s: Responding to Britain's desire to populate Nova Scotia with Protestant Europeans, more than 2,000 "foreign Protestants," German and Swiss colonists settle in Nova Scotia, at present-day Lunenburg.

1759-1774: "Planters," Yankee settlers with farming predilections, are enticed to Nova Scotia, promised free religion and freer land.

Bio JOSEPH HOWE

Joseph Howe was born in Halifax in 1804 to a humble Loyalist family engaged in the printing trade. By the age of 13, Howe and his oldest brother joined the family printing business. At the age of 24, Howe purchased the most important colonial newspaper, *The Nova Scotian*. It was a decision that would change his life and the life of his province forever.

Always interested in politics, in 1835 Howe's paper published a letter critical of the fiscal abuses of the local government and alleged that £30,000 was "taken from the pockets of the people." At the time, the publishing of such an incendiary article was susceptible to charges of criminal libel, and Howe was inevitably charged and stood trial. Taking the stand in his own defense, Howe delivered to the court a six-hour rousing speech in which he not only spoke in his own defense, but in defense of the very principle of freedom of the press.

Riding high on his public popularity after winning the case, Howe was elected to the Nova Scotia House of Assembly the next year. He was soon made leader of the Liberal party and set about ushering in a series of government reforms, known collectively as Howe's "12 Resolutions." The reforms essentially tempered the power of aristocratic, colonial politicians, transferring some of it to the people.

In 1848, thanks to Howe's leadership, Nova Scotia became the first British colony to achieve responsible government. Less successful was Howe's anti-confederation campaign. Staunchly opposed to union with Canada, Howe feared that it would undermine a grander British Empire. He also opposed confederation on practical terms. With eerie foresight, he believed that the terms of union would crush the economy of Nova Scotia.

Howe, however, could stave off neither his political opponent, Charles Tupper, nor the push to union. The year after the 1867 union, Howe continued to oppose it and fought in vain for repeal. With the cause lost, Howe was eventually persuaded to go to Ottawa to join in the building of the new country.

1773: The famed ship Hector lands at Pictou, bringing 189 Scottish settlers to "New Scotland."

1770s-1780s: The "Great Awakening" stirs Nova Scotia when Henry Alline, a young Nova Scotian with a flare for the dramatic, preaches his evangelical message to throngs of excitement starved Nova Scotians, stirring a Christian revival in the fledgling colony and establishing here the roots of a strong Baptist tradition.

1775-1783: When the American Revolution erupts in 1775, Nova Scotia's transplanted Yankees bring great relief to British officials when they do not support their rebelling homeland, but opt instead to become the "neutral Yankees."

1783: When 30,000 colonists loyal to the British Crown are forced to flee the Thirteen Colonies, a diverse group of 19,000 Loyalists, including 1,500 Free Black Loyalists, settle in Nova Scotia, creating a massive logistics headache for colonial officials, and hardship for the Acadians and Natives told to "shove off" to make way for the Loyalists.

1784: Nova Scotia is partitioned into three colonies: Nova Scotia, New Brunswick, and Cape Breton.

1792: Unfair treatment prompts approximately 1,200 Black Loyalists to leave Nova Scotia for Sierra Leone, Africa.

1796: Approximately 500 Maroons sail from Jamaica to make a home in Halifax. Four years later, the government encourages them to relocate to Sierra Leone in order to avoid maintenance costs. The group obliges.

1813-1815: Approximately 2,000 Black refugees trickle into Nova Scotia after the War of 1812.

1820: Cape Breton loses its independent colonial status and (reluctantly) rejoins Nova Scotia.

1848: Nova Scotia becomes the first British colony to get responsible government.

1850-1880: Nova Scotians prosper, engaged in the shipbuilding and shipping industry in the "golden age" of sail.

1864: Although Nova Scotian delegates attend the Charlottetown Conference prepared to consider "Maritime Union," no deal could be reached. The meetings conclude with a proposal for Confederation which is hammered out a month later in Quebec. Anti-Confederates led by Joseph Howe strongly opposed the "Quebec resolutions" while pro-Confederate Charles Tupper called for their adoption.

1867: Nova Scotia becomes part of Canadian Confederation but "better terms" is the rallying cry of disaffected Nova Scotians who felt forced into Confederation.

1892: Nova Scotia-born John Thompson is Canada's fourth Prime Minister.

1912: The majestic Titanic sinks off the Atlantic coast on her maiden voyage. Of the 2,227 passengers and crew on board, there are only 705 survivors. The search effort is coordinated from Halifax and nearly half of the recovered bodies are later buried in the city's cemeteries.

1914-1918: As World War I rages, almost 3,500 Nova Scotians and Prince Edward Islanders (the provinces are grouped together by the Department of Veteran Affairs) pay the ultimate price.

1917: The French munitions ship, the Mont Blanc, collides in Halifax Harbour with the Imo, a Norwegian registered freighter chartered to the Belgian relief effort. The collision detonates 2,653,115 kg of explosives, making it the most powerful non-atomic, manmade blast in history. Almost 2,000 people are killed and property damage is estimated at $35 million (or $430 million in today's currency).

1918: Women in Nova Scotia get the right to vote provincially and federally.

1921: The original Bluenose is launched from a wharf in Lunenburg. The ship sinks off of Haiti in 1946.

1937: The Canadian Mint first emblazons the Canadian dime with the Bluenose image.

1939-45: Almost 60,000 Nova Scotia men enlist in the Canadian armed forces, and 2,525 die in battle.

1954: Nova Scotia is permanently connected to Cape Breton Island with the completion of the Canso Causeway.

1957: Twenty-two scientists from ten nations converge on Pugwash, Nova Scotia to discuss nuclear disarmament, establishing the "Pugwash Conferences" as ongoing international meetings aimed at "reducing the danger of armed conflict and seeking cooperative solutions for global problems."

1958: The Number Four mine at the Cumberland Rail & Coal Co. in Springhill, Nova Scotia experiences a "bump," trapping 174 men 13,000 feet underground for eight days, while the world watched. Tragically, 75 miners are killed.

Take 5 BRUCE NUNN'S
FIVE BEST-KEPT SECRETS IN NOVA SCOTIA

By Bruce Nunn, AKA 'Mr. Nova Scotia Know-It-All', author of *History with a Twist, More History with a Twist, 59 Stories; Nova Scotia's Curious Connections to the Remarkable, the World-Famous and the Strange*; also *The Magical Christmas Light of Old Nova Scotia, Buddy the Bluenose Reindeer,* and *Buddy the Bluenose Reindeer and the Boston Christmas Tree Adventure*. Here, he lets the cat out of the bag on five of Nova Scotia's best-kept secrets.

1. **Bluenose brain:** Nova Scotia's Simon Newcomb, an ingenious astronomer from Cumberland County, recorded mathematical calculations of Mercury's orbit that were cited by Albert Einstein to support and defend his new revolutionary theory of relativity.

2. **Film fame:** Wallace (Wheeler) MacDonald of Mulgrave, N.S., was one of the iconic Keystone Kops in the first ever comedy feature, *Tillie's Punctured Romance*, starring Charlie Chaplin. He also directed some Three Stooges films and had a minor role in *Gold Diggers of 1933*, starring another Nova Scotian actor, Ruby Keeler of Dartmouth.

3. **Legally plaid:** The Nova Scotia Tartan Act makes it illegal to produce or sell the famed blue tartan without a license. The first one issued was #NS1-double-O-1. Double O? Ah yes, a license to kilt!

4. **CSI Halifax:** DNA (deoxyribonucleic acid) was discovered to be the biological blueprint of all life by scientist Oswald Avery who was born and lived as a young boy on Moran St., just north of Citadel Hill in Halifax, Nova Scotia.

5. **Dirt delivery:** A patch of earth at Edinburgh Castle was declared Nova Scotian soil as a spot to dub early investors in New Scotland as 'Baronets of Nova Scotia'. In 1953, N.S. Premier Angus L. Macdonald personally delivered a container of actual bluenose soil to that spot to make it official.

1962: Halifax approves a plan for the destruction of the community of Africville. Demolition is complete by 1967, and former residents are paid a measly $500 for their 'troubles'.

1962: Nova Scotia mall rats rejoice as the province becomes home to the Halifax Shopping Center, North America's second air-conditioned shopping mall.

1983: Prince Charles and his wife Princess Diana of Wales, newly a mother to the heir to the throne of England, visit Nova Scotia.

1983: The Black Cultural Centre for Nova Scotia opens.

1984: Pope John Paul II visits Nova Scotia.

1992: On May 9th at 5:18 am, the Westray coal mine explodes, killing 26 miners.

1995: The G7 Summit, featuring G7 leaders and a wobbly Boris Yeltsin, is held in Halifax in June.

1998: En route from New York City to Geneva, Switzerland, Swiss Air Flight 111 plunges into the Atlantic off Nova Scotia, killing all 215 passengers and 14 crew members.

2001: When terrorists attack the United States, North American air space is closed. Forty diverted planes land at Halifax International Airport. Nova Scotians open their homes and hearts to over 7,000 stranded passengers.

2004: Acadians from around the world gather in Nova Scotia to celebrate the arrival of the first French settlers in Canada four hundred years earlier.

2004: Same-sex marriages are made legal after the Supreme Court of Nova Scotia rules that banning them is unconstitutional.

2005: Sydney Crosby from Cole Harbour is picked first overall in the NHL Entry Draft by the Pittsburgh Penguins. Crosby is touted as the next Wayne Gretzky.

2006: The Supreme Court of Nova Scotia strikes down a law preventing stores from selling goods on Sundays after Sobeys and Atlantic Superstore grocery chains challenged the provincial government. This opened the doors for "Sunday shopping" in all retail locations.

2006: War Brides, women who Canadian soldiers met and brought back to Canada while fighting World War II in Europe, from all over Canada arrive by train at Pier 21 to commemorate "The Year of the War Bride." It was the original point of entry to the country for more than 50,000 women over 60 years ago.

2008: Christa and Joseph MacKinnon of Greenwood really beat the odds by one in 70 million when she gives birth to a set of identical twin boys and a set of identical twin girls in January.

Nova Scotia Essentials

Origin of Name: Latin for "New Scotland." In 1621, King James I of England (James VI of Scotland) claimed the land as a part of the kingdom of Scotland.

Provincial Capital: Halifax

License Plate: "Canada's Ocean Playground" was adopted on the Nova Scotia license plate in 1972.

Motto: *Munit Haec et Altera Vincit* (One defends and the other conquers.)

Bluenosers: There is a great deal of debate about exactly why Nova Scotians are called Bluenosers. Some say it's because the sailors' mittens were blue and the dye got on their noses when they rubbed them; others, because Nova Scotians' noses turned blue from the cold. And one story has it that the nickname was given to the crewmen of schooners that carried blue-skinned Nova Scotia potatoes to New England in the late 1700s. Regardless of the origin, the term is not derisive. Indeed, Nova Scotia's most famous schooner was called the Bluenose.

They said it

Coat of Arms: At the centre on a shield is the provincial flag (a combination of St. Andrew's Cross and the Royal Arms of Scotland). To the left of the arms is a unicorn while a seventeenth century approximation of a native North American stands to the right. The motto, written in Latin above reads "One defends and the other conquers," which is illustrated directly below with two hands shaking; one, bare, holds a laurel branch, symbolizing peace, while the other, clad in armour, holds the thistle of Scotland. At the base is Nova Scotia's floral emblem, the Mayflower, entwined with the thistle of Scotland, which was added in 1929.

Tartan: The blue and white in the tartan stand for the sea; the green represents the forests; red for the royal lion on the shield of arms; and gold for the royal charter of the province.

Provincial Flag: The province's flag is the flag of Scotland with the colours reversed. The "Arms" (the lion rampant) in the center of the flag is a symbol of the crown. Nova Scotia is the first overseas British colony to receive its own flag.

Provincial Flower: Nova Scotia was the first province to adopt a flower. The mayflower, named because it blooms in May, was officially designated in 1901. The mayflower is a spicy-smelling pale pink/white flower that grows in clusters on a shrub.

Provincial Bird: The osprey was designated the official bird of Nova Scotia in 1994. There are 250 active osprey nests in the province.

Provincial Dog: Nova Scotia's official dog, the Duck Tolling Retriever, is native to Yarmouth County. Also known as the Little River Duck Dog, the Toller was recognized as a pure breed by the Canadian Kennel Club in 1945.

Provincial Berry: The blueberry was officially designated our provincial berry in 1996. Nova Scotia is Canada's top producer of blueberries. The town of Oxford calls itself the Blueberry Capital of Canada.

Provincial Tree: The most common tree species in Nova Scotia, the red spruce, became the province's official tree in 1998. It grows to a height of 25 m and its lifespan can reach 400 years.

Time Zone: Atlantic

Area Code: 902

System of Measurement: Metric

Voting Age: 18

Take 5 **TOP FIVE LARGEST**
CITIES AND TOWNS (POPULATION)

1. **Halifax Regional Municipality** (372,679)
2. **Cape Breton Regional Municipality** (102,250)
3. **Truro** (11,765)
4. **Amherst** (9,505)
5. **New Glasgow** (9,455)

Source: Stats Can Community Profiles

Statutory Holidays: Nova Scotia has five official statutory holidays — New Year's Day, Good Friday, Canada Day, Labour Day, and Christmas Day. Most employers also recognize Victoria Day, Thanksgiving, Remembrance Day, Boxing Day, and the first Monday in August.

AMALGAMATION

During the 1990s, the provincial government developed a strategy for municipal restructuring that created large regional governments out of the smaller municipalities of Halifax and Sydney and their environs. In 1995, the Cape Breton Regional Municipality (CBRM) was formed through an amalgamation of eight former municipalities, boards, and agencies within the County of Cape Breton. The following year, the cities of Halifax and Dartmouth, the town of Bedford and the Halifax County Municipality were combined to create the Halifax Regional Municipality (HRM).

SISTER CITIES

Halifax, Nova Scotia's capital, has three sister cities: Hakodate, Japan; Halifax, UK; and Norfolk, USA.

POPULATION BREAKDOWN

Total Population: 913,462
Male: 48.1 percent
Female: 51.9 percent
Rural: 406,530
Urban: 506,932

Source: Stats Can

Did you know...

that Nova Scotia was once a part of the county of Edinburgh, Scotland? In 1621, Sir William Alexander, wanting to claim the province as part of his territory, declared it part of his barony of Edinburgh.

Did you know...

that the first reported quintuplets in Canada were born at Little Egypt, Pictou County in 1880? The three girls and two boys all died within two days.

POPULATION DENSITY (PEOPLE/KM^2)

Alberta: 5.1
Ontario: 13.9
Nova Scotia: 17.8
Prince Edward Island: 23.9
Saskatchewan: 1.7
Toronto: 3,972
New York City: 10,194

Source: aapinfoweb

POPULATION IN PERSPECTIVE

Nova Scotia is more than twice the size of Massachusetts but there are seven times more people in Massachusetts than here. As a percentage of the Canadian populace, the population of both Nova Scotia and Atlantic Canada has been decreasing for more than 60 years as native Nova Scotians leave the province to look for better opportunities and other provinces attract more immigrants. Nova Scotia today accounts for just three percent of the Canadian population.

Take 5 TOP FIVE BABY NAMES
IN NOVA SCOTIA

Boys:
1. Ryan
2. Jacob
3. Ethan
4. Noah
5. Liam

Girls:
1. Emma
2. Ava
3. Madison
4. Olivia
5. Hannah

You Know You're From

- You've worn shorts and a parka at the same time.
- Driving is better in the winter because the potholes are covered with snow.
- Everyone is a fiddle player.
- You can pretend you have Scottish heritage as an excuse to wear a kilt.
- The statement "Can I have a poutine with my donair" doesn't confuse you.
- You understand there's nothing wrong with eating Beaver Tails at the Halifax Waterfront.
- Your grandfather was either a fisherman, a farmer, or a coal miner.
- You automatically assume someone who's rude must be from Toronto or the United States.
- If asked, you give directions in time rather than distance.
- You say hello to someone and they say hello back to you.
- You go for a 2-hour hike in November and hit rain, sleet, snow and sunshine before you get back.
- Someone in a Home Depot store offers you assistance but they don't work there.
- You've had a lengthy telephone conversation with someone who dialed a wrong number.
- "Vacation" means going anywhere beyond Amherst for the weekend.
- You know several people who have hit a deer more than once.
- You have switched from "heat" to "A/C" in the same day and back again.
- You install security lights on your house and garage, but leave both unlocked.
- You design your kid's Halloween costume to fit over a snowsuit.
- You know all 4 seasons: almost winter, winter, still winter and road

Nova Scotia When...

construction.

- You have more miles on your snow blower than your car.
- You find 0°C "a little chilly."
- You think of New Brunswick as the place you have to go through to get anywhere.
- You see cars stop on the street to let pedestrians cross.
- The bars outnumber the citizens by 3 to 1.
- You can wear jeans to ANY restaurant in the province and not look out of place.
- You don't go for coffee, you go for a Timmie's.
- You understand what "sunny breaks" means.
- You know more people who own boats than who have air conditioners.
- You know more people who heat with wood than with oil.
- You can taste the difference between Starbucks, Tim Horton's, and Wendy's coffee.
- You know how to pronounce Tatamagouche, Musquodoboit, and Kejimkujik.
- In winter, you go to work in the dark and come home in the dark while only working eight-hour days.
- You never go camping without waterproof matches and a poncho.
- You are not fazed by "Today's forecast: showers followed by rain," and "Tomorrow's forecast: rain followed by showers."
- You have no concept of humidity without precipitation.
- You put on your shorts when the temperature gets above 10°C, but still wear your sweater and boots.
- 15°C is sandal weather.
- You know people who use umbrellas are either wimps or tourists.
- You buy new sunglasses every year, because you cannot find the old ones after such a long time.

NOT IN THE MILLION CLUB

Although Nova Scotia's population continues to increase, it is increasing at a decreasing rate. If current birth and out-migration patterns continue, the province is not expected to break the million-people barrier. By 2026, after peaking at 950,300, the population is predicted to begin decreasing.

Source: NS Statistical Review

BOYS AND GIRLS

- Median age of Nova Scotian women: 42.5
- Men: 41.1
- Life expectancy of Nova Scotian women: 81.6
- Men: 76.5
- Fertility rate (number of children a woman will have during her lifetime): 1.37

Source: Stats Can

CENTURY CLUB

Some of them attribute it to the sea air; others, to simply minding their own business. Whatever the cause, Nova Scotia has a population of people over the age of 100 that is seven times the world average. On the southwestern coast of Nova Scotia that jumps even higher, to 17 times the world average.

Researchers looking into the phenomenon have noticed that Nova Scotians often speak about very aged relatives, and one researcher even noted that there seems to be an obituary of a centenarian in the newspaper at least once every five or six weeks.

In the end, researchers suspect the combination of an active lifestyle, healthy eating and good genetics plays a role in Nova Scotians living to a great old age. The high population of centenarians along the South Shore may also be attributable to the limited genetic make up of the area. This region is still largely descended from German immigrants who settled the area in the mid-eighteenth century, maintaining the propensity to long life within the local gene pool.

THE MARRYING KIND

The average age of first marriage in Nova Scotia is 29.0 for brides and 30.9 years of age for grooms. Compare that to 30 years ago, when the ages were 21.1 years for women and 23.1 years for men.

Source: Service Nova Scotia Annual Report

FAMILY STRUCTURE

- Percentage of married couple families: 70
- Common law, two-parent families: 13
- Female lone-parent families: 14
- Male lone-parent families: 3

Take 5 SPRING GARDEN ROAD MEMORIAL PUBLIC LIBRARY'S
TOP FIVE ESSENTIAL READS

As the largest branch of the Halifax Public Libraries, the Spring Garden Road Memorial Public Library houses an extensive and in-depth collection of materials and serves as a resource for the region. The branch receives 8,000 visits per week to access its wide-ranging and innovative programs, collections and specialized services. Joanne McCarthy is a librarian specializing in local history and genealogy. Kristina Parlee is a librarian specializing in internationaland regional fiction. Their top five contemporary picks of Nova Scotia must-reads are as follows.

1. *An Illustrated History of Nova Scotia*, by Harry Bruce (1997)

2. *The Nova Scotia Phrase Book: Sayings, Expressions, and Odd Names of Nova Scotia*, by Dan Soucoup (2007)

3. *Nova Scotia Landmarks*, by Len Wagg (2004)

4. *To Find Us: Words and Images of Halifax*, edited by Sue MacLeod (2005)

5. *No Great Mischief*, by Alistair MacLeod (1999)

D-I-V-O-R-C-E
- Divorce rate (per 100,000) in Nova Scotia: 28.9
- Divorce rate in Canada: 38.3
- Divorce rate in Quebec, the highest in Canada: 49.7
- Divorce rate in Newfoundland and Labrador, the lowest: 17.1

AGE STRUCTURE
- Percentage of population that is under 25: 29.9 percent
- Ages 25 - 44: 26.5 percent
- Ages 45 - 65: 29.4 percent
- Ages 65+: 15.1 percent

Source: Stats Can

ON A TYPICAL DAY IN NOVA SCOTIA . . .
- 23 children are born
- 22 people die
- 13 marriages take place, 5 in civil ceremonies and 8 by religious clergy
- 5 people divorce

FAMILY STRUCTURE
- Number of all families (married and common law, single parent): 267,415
- Percentage of married couple families with children: 36
- Percentage of married couple families without children: 34
- Percentage of common law families with children: 5

Did you know...

that Nova Scotia was the sixth province/territory in Canada, and the first in Atlantic Canada, to legalize same-sex marriage?

Did you know...

that every 122 days in Nova Scotia, a marriage takes place in which both parties are teenagers?

Higher Education

Nova Scotia has 11 world-class universities offering a wide range of programs at the bachelor, masters and doctoral levels.

- Dalhousie University (15,000 full time students) is the largest university in the Maritimes and probably the most well known.
- University of King's College (1,100 students) is the oldest university in Canada. King's is best known for its Foundation Year and Journalism programs.
- Saint Mary's University (8,800 students) is home of the Huskies and one of the best football programs in Canada. SMU offers programs in business, astronomy and international development studies, to name a few.
- Mount Saint Vincent University (2,300 full time students) was a women-only school until 1967. The Mount offers degrees in a variety of disciplines but is noted for its information technology and public relations programs.
- Nova Scotia College of Art and Design (over 1,000 students) is an art school with an international reputation. NSCAD (pronounced "nascad") is the alma mater of singer Sarah McLachlan.
- Acadia University (3,000 full time students) is best known for pioneering the integration of laptop computers into the school computers and counts Canadian Defense Minister Peter Mackay amongst its alumni.
- Saint Francis Xavier University (4,200 students) in Antigonish was named *MacLean's* top primarily undergraduate school five years running between 2002 and 2006. Alumni from Saint FX can be recognized by their 'X Rings' emblazoned with a large black X.
- There is also the Nova Scotia Agricultural College in Truro, the Atlantic School of Theology in Halifax, Cape Breton University in Sydney and the province's only French school, Universite Sainte-Anne.
- The Nova Scotia Community College is the province's largest college with 10,000 students spread out over 13 campuses.

Source: http://www.novascotiaeducation.com.

- Single parent (male): 3
- Single parent (female): 14

RELIGIOUS AFFILIATION

Roman Catholicism is the largest religious denomination in Nova Scotia,
but the combined Protestant denominations outnumber Catholics.

- Percentage of Nova Scotians who are Protestant: 49
- Roman Catholic: 37
- Muslim: 0.4
- Jewish: 0.2
- Hindu: 0.1
- Buddhist: 0.2
- Of no religious affiliation: 12

Source: NS Statistical Review

LANGUAGES SPOKEN

- Percentage of Nova Scotians whose mother tongue is English: 92.1
- French: 3.6
- Arabic: 0.49
- Mi'kmaq: 0.45
- German: 0.45
- Percentage who are bilingual (English and French): 10.3

Did you know...

FULL-TIME STUDENTS ENROLLED
Universities: 35,772
Colleges (Provincial): 9,922
Other colleges: 2,330
Public schools: 138,661
Private or independent schools: 6,735

Source: NS Department of Finance, Economics and Statistics Division

HEALTH CARE PROFESSIONALS
Physicians: 2,247
Dentists: 517
Nurses: 9,422
Pharmacists: 1,096

Weblinks

Nova Scotia's Official Tourism Website
www.novascotia.com
Tour the Cabot Trail, watch the high tides at the Bay of Fundy, explore Peggy's Cove, take a whale watching trip, enjoy waterfront dining, attend one of over 700 festivals — find out what's going on here.

The Chronicle Herald
www.thechronicleherald.ca
The best source of local news in Nova Scotia, featuring articles from The *Chronicle Herald*, breaking news, sports, entertainment, business, national news, and more.

Nova Scotia Education
www.novascotiaeducation.com
This website, also known as "Canada's Education Province," gives up the goods if you're looking at furthering your education close to home.

Place Names

The names of places provide us with clues about a history that often remains unknown or is merely speculated upon by visitors or even by its own residents. What the origins of a name reveal can be a place in time, a geographical feature (often lost because of development), or the importance of the naming people. What they've provided Nova Scotians with is a rich treasure of colourful historical markers.

Amherst, Cumberland County: A Mi'kmaq name for it was Nemcheboogwek, meaning "going up rising ground." The town's first name was Les Planches, given by an Acadian settlement in 1672. The French put the village to the torch in 1755. In 1759, the town was given its current name in honour of Lord Jeffrey Amherst, who captured Louisbourg in 1758 in co-operation with Admiral Boscawen.

Annapolis Royal, Annapolis County: This place had two Mi'kmaq names: Esunuskek, meaning "hard ground and well swarded," and Eisuneskwek, meaning "Eison's place." After the basin's discovery by the French in 1604, it took on the name Port Royal. It was later changed to Annapolis after Queen Anne when the fort was captured by the English in 1710.

Antigonish, Antigonish County: A Mi'kmaq word with two meanings; "where branches are torn off" or "river of fish."

Baddeck, Victoria County: A derivation of the Mi'kmaq name Abadak or Abadek, meaning two completely different things: "a portion of food set aside for someone" or "a sultry place."

Bedford, Halifax County: First called Sackville, this city was later named in honour of John Russell, the fourth Duke of Bedford (1710-1771). He was First Lord of the Admiralty and was Secretary of State for the colonies during the founding of Halifax. Before the 20th century, people also called Bedford the "Ten-Mile House," because it was ten miles from an Inn where stage coaches stopped to change horses and where sleighing parties from the city came for entertainment.

Canso, Guysborough County: Western Europeans were fishing in the area for years prior to when French fisherman established a settlement in 1604. The name comes from the Mi'kmaq word Kamsok, which means "opposite the lofty cliffs." The Canso crater on Mars is named for the town.

Chegoggin, Yarmouth County: This comes from a Mi'kmaq word that meant "great encampment." Another meaning, Isagoggin, means "the place for weirs."

Chezzetcook, Halifax County: A variation of the Mi'kmaq name Chesetkook or Sesetkook. These words mean "flowing rapidly in many channels." The name may have also come from the French saying, chez les coques, meaning "home of the sea birds."

Cogmagun, Hants County: An English take on the Mi'kmaq word Kogumegunuk or Kookemagun, which is said to mean "the crooked river."

Dartmouth, Halifax County: The Mi'kmaq name was Boonamoogwaddy, meaning "Tomcod ground." There are two possible explanations for the English name. First is that it could have been given in honour of William Legge, Earl of Dartmouth, Colonial Secretary from 1772-75. The other, and the more probable of the two, is that it was named for the Devonshire Port of Dartmouth.

Digby, Digby County: The Mi'kmaq name for this settlement was Oositookun, meaning "an ear." The first English name for it was Conway, given in 1766 by English settlers from Brandywine in New England and a group that moved from Annapolis. The current name was decided by a large group of Loyalists in 1783 that arrived from New England. The name is in honour of Admiral Robert Digby.

Take 5 FIVE THINGS TO DO FOR FREE IN NOVA SCOTIA

The staff members of Halifax Waterfront Visitor's Information Centre, located at Sackville Landing, put their heads together and came up with their five favourite free things to do in the province for visitors and locals alike.

1. **Provincial Parks:** Provincial parks throughout the province offer free access to hiking trails, picnic sites and beaches.
2. **Lighthouses:** Lighthouses like Cape d'Or near Advocate Harbour and Cape Forchu in Yarmouth.
3. **Peggy's Cove:** Peggy's Cove Lighthouse in a quaint fishing village is also a post office set in the midst of a natural and geological marvel.
4. **Tidal Bores:** The Tidal Bore at Truro, South Maitland or Windsor.
5. **Beautiful Falls:** The scenery and changing autumn colours.

Ecum Secum, Halifax County: This name has been in the making since 1809. The word used that year was Ekemsagen, while an 1813 variation was Ekemsikam. By 1845, the well-known "Ecum Secum" spelling was used. The Mi'kmaq name for it was Megwasaagunk or Agwasaagunk, meaning "a red house" or "a red bank."

Warden of the North

In 1749, 37-year-old Edward Cornwallis brought an estimated 2,500 English men and women, mostly Londoners, to this rocky, untouched land. Cornwallis was shrewd enough to name his new settlement in honour of his patron, George Dunk, Earl of Halifax and chief lord of trade and plantations. What Cornwallis seemed less concerned about was whether his new settlers had enough time to put together suitable digs to make it through a Canadian winter.

They didn't, and it is estimated that upwards of 1,000 of them perished trying to stay warm and keep dissolute soldiers at bay. Cornwallis ended his days in the warmth of Gibraltar. The new settlers, the ones that made it through that mad winter, must have surprised even themselves when in the spring that followed they began to carve out the beginnings of a community from the forested hillside.

By 1828, when Nova Scotia's most famous patriot, Joseph Howe, was purchasing the Halifax newspaper that would make him famous, Halifax's population had ballooned to 14,500, 1,800 of whom were members of the garrison. It was the center of its own universe, and if it looked anywhere for some party to acknowledge its growing importance it was to London.

Halifax was a determined upstart wanting to do the Empire proud. There was, of course, another Halifax, just like there was another London, one that Dickens would capture so brilliantly. There was, indeed, enterprise and opportunity in Halifax, but there was also poverty and squalor of Dickensian proportions. On a single street,

Garden of Eden, Pictou County: William MacDonald, one of the first settlers around the year 1830, named this place after the biblical garden because of its intense beauty. It is located on the Moose River, on the north side of Eden Lake.

Albermarle Street of the 1850s, there were more than a hundred rum shops, and upwards of 600 women engaged in prostitution.

When Canada came calling in 1867, Howe and the majority of Nova Scotians wanted no part of it. Howe envisioned greatness for his little city and province, and that greatness was not going to be achieved by going to Ottawa. In 1867, Howe made the long steam to London one last time.

He was convinced that he could prevail upon Westminster to scrap its plans for the new country they were about to create. In the end, what Howe witnessed first hand was the passage of the Constitution Act without a murmur of debate. To add insult to injury, the legislation that followed — a bill dealing with untended dogs on London's streets — stirred British passions more than the creation of a new country of which he was now inextricably bound.

Apart from interludes during the war years, Halifax has not pulsed with the same mercantile optimism since the 1870s. The merchants and the hustlers have been replaced by the professional classes. Doctors, lawyers, teachers, and especially bureaucrats, have come to succeed them.

Halifax, of course, is no longer a colonial town. The vestiges of the Empire are in the buildings and parks and gardens. The people here have created their own culture and it is a thriving one. The city has a uniqueness and a delightful rough and bawdy edge that has given it a character that anybody spending time here will come to recognize.

They said it

Grand Pre, Kings County: Originally settled by Acadians who were later expelled, the name is a French word meaning "great meadow."

Halifax, Halifax County: The Mi'kmaq name for Nova Scotia's capital was Chebookt, meaning "Chief Harbour" or "Great Long Harbour." The English name was in honour of George Montagu Dunk, second Earl of Halifax and president of the Board of Trade and Plantations at the time.

Havre Boucher, Antigonish County: The town is named for the bay on which it is situated. The bay was named after Quebecer Captain Francis Boucher, who spent the winter there in 1759 after his ship was caught in the ice.

Kentville, Kings County: This English name was given in honour of the Duke of Kent in 1826, who had visited the settlement in 1794. The Mi'kmaq name was Penooek, meaning "Pineo's Place."

Did you know...

that the Halifax Regional Municipality is the fifth largest municipality in Canada?

They said it

Lunenburg, Lunenburg County: One of two original Mi'kmaq names was Aseedik, meaning "place of clams." The second was Merliguesene, meaning "milky bay." The current town was established in 1753 and named in honour of the Duke of Braunschweig-Luneburg who was crowned King of England in 1727.

New Minas, Kings County: This settlement received its original name, Les Mines, after French explorers found veins of copper at what they named Cap d'Or on the north side of the basin. Les Mines was changed to Minas.

Necum Teuch, Halifax County: It is said that this name probably means "soft sand place," from the Mi'kmaq name Noogoomkeak.

Nuttby, Colchester County: The name's origin is broken into two parts — "Nutt" is part of the family name, McNutt, and "by" means a dwelling or town. Put them together and you get a dwelling place of the McNutt family!

Did you know...

that inventor Alexander Graham Bell is buried near Baddeck in Cape Breton?

Nyanza, Victoria County: Named after Lake Nyanza in Africa. A Mi'kmaq reservation existed in this town in the early 1900's.

Parrsboro, Cumberland County: This English version was named after John Parr, Governor of Nova Scotia from 1782 to 1791. The Mi'kmaq word for this place is Awokum, meaning "a portage" or "short-cut."

Point Aconi, Cape Breton County: Named for the headland on which it is located. Aconi comes from the Greek word "acon" which means "a dart."

Pubnico, Yarmouth County: From the original Mi'kmaq word, Pogomkook, meaning "land from which the trees have been removed to fit it for cultivation."

Pugwash, Cumberland County: This name originates from the Mi'kmaq word Pagwechk or Pagwesk, meaning "shallow water or shoal." It was once called Waterford.

Did you know...

that the reconstruction of the Port Royal Habitation near Annapolis in 1939-1941 was the very first National Historic Site in Canada to have a replica structure built?

Sackville, Halifax County: The Mi'kmaq name for this place was Aloosoolawakade, meaning "place of measles" after a measles epidemic that killed many. The English name came from Fort Sackville, a military fort started at the head of the Bedford Basin by Captain John Goreham in September 1749 for the protection of Halifax. It is believed that the fort's name came from the Viscount Sackville.

Shinimicas Bridge, Cumberland County: This place name, also spelled as Shinimecas, is a Mi'kmaq name meaning "shining river." It is a community located on the Shinimicas River.

Shubenacadie, Hants County: This place name comes from the Mi'kmaq word Segubunakade meaning "place where ground nuts grow."

Stewiacke, Colchester County: Originated from the Mi'kmaq word Esiktaweak, meaning "it oozed slowly out from still water."

Sydney, Cape Breton County: The Mi'kmaq name for Sydney Harbour was Cibou, meaning river or inlet. The city went through many name changes before it acquired its current one. On Denys' map of 1672, Sydney Harbour is written as "La R. Denys." It was known as Spanish Bay before the end of the 17th century. It was called Dartmouth Harbour in Holland's description of Cape Breton Island. The present name comes from Hon. Thomas Townsend, first Viscount Sydney.

Did you know...

that Paul Revere received a freemasons degree just outside of Yarmouth?

They said it

" . . . the wharfs are crowded with vessels of all kinds discharging their cargoes or taking in the returns. Signals are constantly flying at the citadel for vessels coming in; merchants are running about, in anticipation of their freights; officers of the garrison are seen striding down with a determined pace . . . and ladies, tripping along on the tiptoe of expectation . . . "

– Captain William Moorson, British soldier
in his book *Letters from Nova Scotia*

Tatamagouche, Colchester County: This name evolved from the original Mi'kmaq word Takamegoochk, which means "barred across the entrance with sand."

Truro, Colchester County: Named after Truro in Cornwall, England, remembered for the surrender of Lord Hopton's troops to General Fairfax after the battle of Naseby. The original Mi'kmaq name was Wagobagitzk, meaning "the bay runs far up," or "the end of the waters flow." This name was in reference to the Fundy tides. The French Acadians called it Cobequid, a name that came from the Mi'kmaq word for the same place.

Did you know...

that Windsor, Nova Scotia is considered by many to be the birthplace of hockey?

Washabuck Centre, Victoria County: This name is said to be Mi'kmaq for "an angle of land formed between a river and a lake." There are two other spellings for it — Washabuckt and Astchbuckt. Another name for it is Wosobachuk, meaning "placid water."

Wolfville, Kings County: The Mi'kmaq name for this place was Mtaban, meaning "mud-cat-fish ground." It was first called Mud Creek by the Planters, and in 1829 the prominence of the DeWolf family brought about the current name.

Windsor, Hants County: The Mi'kmaq name for the region was Pesaquid, meaning "junction of waters" referring to the Avon and St. Croix rivers, which flow into the Bay of Fundy. When the French settled the area in 1685 they kept the name. Permanent British settlement began in 1749, when the town was given the name of Windsor.

Yarmouth, Yarmouth County: The area's Mi'kmaq name was Kespoogwit, meaning "land's end," and Yarmouth's name was Maligeak, meaning "crooked every which way." This description referred to the Yarmouth River. Champlain called the place Port Fourchu, "Forked Harbour." This name still applies to Cape Fourchu, on the western side of the harbour. The English name was in use about 1759.

Scotia Slang:
A Dictionary of Nova Scotian English

Every country and region of the world has its own distinct language. Words and expressions have been nurtured and given meaning over time. They inform the jokes we tell and provide us with a shorthand that can only come to be known by living here. Nova Scotia is blessed with a richness of language that can vary from county to county, and of which we can only offer a small sampling here.

Africadia: The term coined by poet, author and black activist, George Elliott Clarke, for Nova Scotia to reflect the social, cultural and economic presence of black people in Nova Scotia, both past and present.

Antis: Nova Scotians who opposed Confederation.

Bass River Chair: A chair made by the Dominion Chair Company at Bass River, Nova Scotia.

Bluenosers: Slang term for Nova Scotians.

Boston States: New England, a region with which Nova Scotians have traditionally had extremely close ties.

Bud/Buddy: A friend, a pal.

Ceilidh: Common to Cape Breton, these are informal social gatherings featuring Scottish/Irish dancing, music and story telling.

Caper: Someone from Cape Breton.

Cheticamp Hookers: Not what you think. These are upstanding Acadian women (and men) who live in Cheticamp, Cape Breton and are known worldwide for their rug-hooking skills.

Come-From-Away: Someone from anywhere but Nova Scotia, especially from outside the Maritimes. (CFA for short.)

Dome, The: The most famous drinking establishment in the province, the Liquor Dome, found in downtown Halifax.

Donair: Something akin to a gyro, this sandwich wrapped in pita bread features spicy meat, tomatoes, onions, and a distinctly Nova Scotian sauce which is sweet, creamy and garlicky.

Double-Double: A coffee prepared with two cream and two sugar (see also triple-triple).

Duck Toller: In full, the Nova Scotian Duck Tolling Retriever, a dog bred in Nova Scotia in the early 19th century to "toll," or lure, and retrieve waterfowl.

Dulse: Dried seaweed, enjoyed as a salty snack.

Dumb as a Stump: Stupid.

Eh: A truly Canadian phrase, but in Nova Scotia it has an implicit question mark and means "what?"

Elephant Grass: The Nova Scotian term (especially connected to Annapolis County) for '*Phragmites australis*,' a tall willowy grass, once used by the Acadians to thatch their roofs.

Eureka: Usually a term of exclamation. In Nova Scotia it is a small Pictou County town so-named for the Eureka Milling Company established there in 1883.

Farewell to Nova Scotia: A folk song, and unofficial Nova Scotian anthem.

Fast as Snot: Really, really fast.

Take 5 FIVE "HALIBURTANISMS"
SAYINGS COINED BY NOVA SCOTIA'S T.C. HALIBURTON

Thomas Chandler Haliburton was the toast of the British Empire. His success is said to have inspired another young writer with a similar wit by the name of Mark Twain. In introducing an international audience to a decidedly non-colonial take on life in North America, he created a new vocabulary rich in simile and metaphor that is still with us today. Here are just some examples.

1. **Raining cats and dogs**
2. **Honesty is the best policy**
3. **The early bird catches the worm**
4. **An ounce of prevention is worth a pound of cure**
5. **Jack of all trades and master of none**

Feed of Smelts: A springtime ritual - a feast of the fresh water fish called smelts.

Frenchys: A phenomenally successful chain of stores in Nova Scotia that sells used clothing from the Boston States.

Going Down the Road: Literally, going down the road, but this phrase mainly refers to people who are leaving the province to find work elsewhere, traditionally in Upper Canada, but more recently includes places like Alberta.

Giv'er: "Go for it."

Haligonian: Someone from the provincial capital, Halifax.

Hodge Podge: A Nova Scotian delicacy consisting of new garden vegetables boiled and bathed in cream.

HRM: The Halifax Regional Municipality, the amalgamated provincial capital (1996) consisting of the communities of Halifax, Dartmouth, Bedford and Sackville, as well as the county of Halifax.

Hurley: An early incarnation of hockey, played with a ball, not a puck, at Windsor, the birthplace of hockey.

Keith's: Properly, "Alexander Keith's Pale Ale," a popular beer made in Nova Scotia.

Kitchen Party: An informal gathering of friends and family which inevitably ends up in the kitchen, the focal point of Nova Scotian social life.

The L.C.: The Liquor Commission, where Nova Scotians buy their beer, such as Keith's, as well as wine and spirits.

Les Suetes: Southeasterly winds known to be especially fierce at Cheticamp, Cape Breton. Known to reach hurricane strength, these winds are often damaging, and warrant weather warnings. They are created when warm air moves over cool water. This front inversion creates a "funneling effect" over elevations like the Cape Breton Highlands and the air is forced to speed up, creating strong gusts as it comes down the side of the elevation.

Take 5 ANNE SIMPSON'S
FIVE PHRASES THAT DESCRIBE NOVA SCOTIA

What words would an award-winning poet use to describe Nova Scotia? This is the question we asked Anne Simpson of Antigonish. Her most recent collection of poems, *Loop*, won the country's most prestigious poetry prize in 2004, the $40,000 Griffin Poetry Prize. She is also author of the novel, *Canterbury Beach*, and another book of poetry, *Light Falls Through You*, winner of the Atlantic Poetry Prize. Simpson has lived in France and in Italy and worked for two years as a teacher in Nigeria before moving to Nova Scotia about 15 years ago. Today she teaches part-time at St. Francis Xavier University, where she also co-ordinates the Great Blue Heron Writing Workshop. In 2005-2006 she was also the writer-in-residence for the Pictou Antigonish Regional Library.

1. a glide of eagles over Monk's Head
2. yellow-gold leaves — an old tree, wakened
3. threaded through snow, a whisky-coloured stream
4. now the dancers: five deer
5. home, the scent of bread

MacPass: Electronic pass purchased, in lieu of using tokens or quarters, to facilitate crossing the Macdonald Bridge that connects Halifax and Dartmouth.

Me Son: Term of endearment, given by an elderly man in reference to a younger man (a literal kinship is not necessary).

Men of the Deeps: Generically, miners who toil in Cape Breton Coal mines, and also a world-renowned choir consisting of the same name.

Mi-Carême: This Cape Breton mid-Lent celebration, adapted from ancient French custom, is designed to ease the drudgery of Lenten sacrifice. During Mi-Carême, people don costumes and visit their friends and families, who have to guess the identities of those in disguise.

Mug up: An evening cup o'tea.

NBA: In the perennial battle between CFAs (Come-From-Aways) and the local population, a CFA can respond — and often does — by calling the locals "NBAs" . . . Never-Been-Aways.

Nor'Easter: A strong coastal storm that requires cold air meeting warm, a source of moisture and a strong jet stream.

Oat Cakes: A hearty oat cookie, also called "Scotch Cakes."

Pizza Corner: A haven for pizza lovers in Halifax, this corner of the city at Blowers and Grafton Streets features three pizza joints at one intersection. The fourth corner offers a stone wall on which to sit and eat!

Poutine Râpée: Unlike the Quebec-originated concoction of french fries, cheese curds and gravy, this Acadian poutine is a baseball-sized ball of grated and mashed potato that is salted, stuffed with pork, boiled, then served with salt and pepper or brown sugar.

Rappie Pie: An Acadian comfort food, this is a dish of grated potatoes and stewed chicken.

Rear: A meaning of this word unique to Nova Scotia, especially Cape Breton, is its usage to denote the back section of a community, sections of land often deemed less desirable.

Rummies: Nova Scotians who, in the late nineteenth and early twentieth centuries, opposed the prohibition of alcohol.

Smashers: Nova Scotians who, in the late 19th and early 20th centuries, desired a prohibition on alcohol.

Sociable: A social tradition in Nova Scotian bars. A sociable is the raising of glasses in unison, in response to the cry, "Sociable!"

Sou'Wester: A rain-slicker hat, worn by fishermen.

Seattle East: Halifax, so-named because it, like Seattle, was home to a sizeable grunge music movement in the 1990s.

Skatist: Early Nova Scotian name for a skater.

Tarbish: A card game played primarily by the people in Cape Breton.

Timmy's/Tim's: Tim Hortons, a Canadian coffee shop chain, co-founded by Nova Scotian Ron Joyce from Tatamagouche, with a remarkably abundant Nova Scotia presence.

The Valley: To Nova Scotians, the Annapolis Valley.

Tourtière: A traditional Acadian meat pie, served especially at Christmas.

Trailer Park Boys: A popular TV show set in a trailer park, with something of a cult following. The show, which traces the lives of a pathetic bunch of losers, is filmed in and around Halifax.

Triple-Triple: A coffee prepared with three creams, three sugars. In Nova Scotia this usually happens at Timmy's.

Two-four: A case of twenty-four beers.

Upper Canadian: Often pejorative, someone from Ontario.

White Juan: A term now indelibly ingrained in the Nova Scotia lexicon, this refers to the massive snow storm of February 18-19, 2004, which dropped up to 100 cm of snow on the province and brought fierce winds gusting to 120 km/hr. White Juan was reminiscent of the devastating Hurricane Juan, which tracked across the province the previous September.

Weblinks

Cape Sable Slang, History, and Folklore
www.geocities.com/jeffronr/tourism/csi.html
A charming local website that deciphers the most unique accents in the province.

Canadian Slang and English Words
www.canadaka.net/content/page/124-canadian-slang--english-words
Here you can take a look at slang all across the country – each word tells you where it is used and what it means.

CBC's 5,000 New Words
www.cbc.ca/news/background/language/
CBC designates a web page to define some of the 5,000 new Canadian official words, as appearing in the Canadian Oxford Dictionary.

Natural World

Nova Scotia is the second smallest province in Canada, larger only than Prince Edward Island. Still, it is twice the size of Massachusetts and just a bit smaller than the country of Ireland. Its land mass accounts for 0.6 percent of Canada's total, but then again, Canada is the second largest country in the world behind Russia.

One of Nova Scotia's great historians, J. Murray Beck, describes the province as jutting out into the North Atlantic like some giant lobster-shaped pier. Indeed it is connected to mainland North America by a small isthmus only 24 km across. One-fifth of the province's land mass consists of the island of Cape Breton Island.

SUM IS GREATER THAN THE PARTS

Nova Scotia wasn't Nova Scotia a billion years ago, of course. Nova Scotia was formed as a result of the coming together of a large moun-tainous land mass formed near the equator with another giant land mass with more desert-like qualities, formed 750 million years ago near the current South Pole. The result is that the province is divided in two by a diagonal fault-line that is a result of the coming together.

The real legacy manifests itself in three distinct terrains. First, there are the Atlantic uplands, which stretch all along the southern and eastern coastlines and as far as 80 km inland. Their most striking feature is the rocky coastal shore, full of bays, coves and inlets. A second distinct terrain is the highlands, a series of mountainous regions lying alongside the Bay of Fundy and throughout much of Cape Breton Island. Finally, there are the lowlands of the Annapolis Valley and along the Northumberland Strait, often lying below sea level and forming the most fertile agricultural land in the province.

PHYSICAL SETTING
- Size: 55,490 km^2
- Length: 575 km
- Average width: 128 km
- Furthest distance from the ocean: 56 km
- Length of shoreline: 7,579 km

Take 5 — LANCE MOORE'S TOP 5 BEACHES IN MAINLAND NOVA SCOTIA

Lance Moore is one of Nova Scotia's top surfers and has owned a surf shop since 1992. He currently owns the Dacane Surf Shop in downtown Halifax, which doubles as the unofficial hub of surfing in the area.

1. **Martinique Beach** (Eastern Shore)
2. **Lawrencetown Beach** (Eastern Shore)
3. **Hurdles Beach** (South Shore)
4. **Cherry Hill** (South Shore)
5. **White Point** (South Shore)

LONGITUDE AND LATITUDE

Nova Scotia is located between 43° and 48° north latitude, and between 59° and 67° west longitude. This puts the province halfway between the equator and the North Pole. In fact, with a latitude of 45°08', the town of Stewiacke is almost precisely at the halfway point. On the global grid, Halifax is located at 44 degrees latitude and 63 degrees longitude. This places it on similar latitude lines with cities such as Bangor, Maine, Bucharest in Romania, and Timaru, New Zealand, and on near-par longitude with Porto Velho, Brazil.

PARKS

- Number of provincial parks: 129
- Number of federal parks: 2 (Kejimkujik and the Cape Breton Highlands)
- Area of federal parks: 135,170 ha
- Historic sites: 16 (plus the New England Planters Exhibit and Lunenburg's The Bank Fishery/Age of Sail exhibit which is overseen by Parks Canada)
- Recreation sites: 64

Take 5   TOP FIVE PEAKS
(ALL IN CAPE BRETON)

1. **White Hill** – 536 m
2. **The Pinnacle** – 530 m
3. **Grey Hill** – 464 m
4. **John Peters Mountain** – 457 m
5. **Icy Mountain** – 452 m

SEEING THE TREES FOR THE FOREST

When the first European settlers came to Nova Scotia, the most prominent feature of the land was its dense mixed forests. Today, 77 percent of Nova Scotia's land mass is still woodland, amounting to 4.25 million hectares of forest. About one-fifth of this is Crown land.

- Percentage of forest lands that is softwood: 54
- Hardwood: 13
- Mixed woods: 24
- Other: 9
- Percentage of Nova Scotian forest that is harvested commercially each year: 2
- Percentage of harvested areas that grow back naturally: 85
- Percentage that is reforested using seedlings: 15

MOTHER NATURE'S PRUNING

Every summer Nova Scotians can expect 400 to 500 forest fires. The most destructive forest fire season of recent times was 1976 when 17,536 hectares of forest burned.

FARM COUNTRY

With 77 percent of Nova Scotia covered in trees, three percent in wetlands, and many coastal areas too rocky to grow anything, it leaves only ten percent of provincial lands suitable for agriculture. Three of the most productive areas are the lowlands of the Annapolis Valley, the shores of the Northumberland Strait, and the Margaree Valley in Cape Breton.

Acadian settlers were the first methodical farmers in the province. In the early 1600s they built intricate systems of dykes along the Fundy shore to claim rich, fertile soil from the sea. About 240 km of that dyke system still exists today, protecting 33,000 hectares of land, and over 600 residential and commercial buildings, from the Fundy tides.

Nova Scotia's Most Famous Sandbar

Although most Nova Scotians have never been to Sable Island, it holds a mythical place in their hearts and minds. And little wonder why. It sits in the Atlantic Ocean some 300 km southeast of Halifax, orphaned and with no permanent residents, yet by some historical quirk of fate, 250 horses roam the island freely, persevering and even reveling in its punishing climate.

The crescent shaped island is only 42 km long and 1.5 km wide at its widest. Three major ocean currents — the Labrador, the Belle Isle and the Gulf Stream — converge around it, mixing a brew of warm and cold waters that means it is covered in fog for more than a third of the year.

Adding to Sable's mystique are the more than 350 shipwrecks that have happened off its shores. Sailors, privateers, convicts and pirates have all been temporary residents here. In one incident, forty convicts were shipwrecked here in 1598, and when their rescuers came some five years later that number had shrunk to 12. There has been no accounting of the lives taken by Sable, but in two consecutive years, 1926 and 1927, the Lunenburg fishing fleet alone lost 138 men.

There were many stories told back on land of deliberate wrecks, where "wreckers" crashed their vessels, murdering their passengers only to make away with their valuables. It was these "wreckers" that prompted the government to build the first lighthouse in 1873 (it had to be moved five times because of erosion), and it remained staffed until the 1960s.

Islands have always captured writers' imaginations and Sable is no different. Nova Scotia's most celebrated writer, Thomas Raddall, had worked on Sable Island as a young man, and much of the plot for his book *The Nymph and the Lamp* was set on Sable. Other writers, like Barbara Christie and Marq deVilliers, have followed in Raddall's footsteps.

WATER, WATER EVERYWHERE

ISLANDS
- Number of coastal islands: 3,809
- Percentage of the provincial landmass that is made up of islands: 20
- Percentage of that accounted for by Cape Breton Island: 93

CAPE BRETON
- Length of Cape Breton Island: 175 km
- Width at its widest point: 135 km
- Rank of Cape Breton Island on the list of the largest islands in the world: 75
- Percentage of the Nova Scotia coastline accounted for by Cape Breton Island: 25

Did you know...

that there are more than 300 species of seaweed around Nova Scotia coasts? Seaweed growth occurs most abundantly on the rocky shores of the Atlantic coast. The main seaweeds attaching to rocks are the kelps and rockweeds. Eelgrass prefers the soft bottoms of protected inlets and bays, especially in the Northumberland Strait.

Take 5 — TOP FIVE LONGEST RIVERS
IN NOVA SCOTIA

1. **West River St. Marys** - 118 km
2. **Mersey River** - 115 km
3. **Tusket River** - 112 km
4. **Annapolis River** - 102 km
5. **Medway River** - 100 km

BEACHES

The warmest beaches in Nova Scotia are along the shores of the Northumberland Strait. The waters in the Strait are shallow enough that they heat up faster in the summer than beaches along the Atlantic coast.

- Number of publicly accessible beaches in the province: over 100
- Number of people who visit Nova Scotia's public beaches each year: 250,000-500,000

WATER

- Percentage of the total landmass of Nova Scotia that is fresh water: 3.5
- Number of lakes larger than one hectare: 6,600
- Number of lakes greater than 1,000 square meters: 38,242 lakes + 67 river lakes
- Number of major rivers: 166

Did you know...

that in 1985 the largest fossil find ever in North America was unearthed on the north shore of the Minas Basin, near Parrsboro? More than 100,000 fossil specimens — some more than 200 million years old — were found, including a series of dinosaur footprints, each the size of a penny.

LARGEST . . .

- **LAKE** in the province is Bras d'Or Lake in Cape Breton, which covers about one-tenth of the Island. But being in such close proximity to the ocean, it actually holds salt water, making it the largest saltwater lake in North America.

Take 5 SILVER DONALD'S
FIVE FAVOURITE CAPE BRETON BEACHES

Silver Donald Cameron is one of Nova Scotia's most gifted writers. His books have ranged over subjects as diverse as the fishery and economic development to his award-winning *The Living Beach*. Cameron is an inveterate traveller and has stepped foot on some of the world's best beaches. Here he gives us the low-down on the best beaches on one of the most beautiful islands in the world. Cameron's books are available at Breton Books. Like any shrewd fisherman, though, Cameron ain't telling anyone his favourite beach.

1. **Port Hood**. A classic sandy swimming beach, reached through a municipal park, Port Hood Beach is easily accessible from the Ceilidh Trail, and fronts on the warm salt water of the Gulf of St. Lawrence. Directly across from the beach is Port Hood Island, whose old houses have been preserved as summer homes — and which has beaches equally appealing. Similar beaches extend all along the Gulf shore from the New Brunswick border to Cheticamp.

2. **Point Michaud**. A cold, fog-draped Atlantic beach, Point Michaud is a long arc of fine grey sand backed by low grassy dunes, with only a sprinkling of homes and cottages. Point Michaud itself is a tombolo, an eroding headland connected to the Cape Breton shore by a neck of sand, with beaches on both sides. Gannets fish offshore, and easterly gales create a magnificent surf. The water is often bitingly cold. The main beach is perhaps a mile and a half in length, but even on a hot Canada Day fewer than 100 people were frisking on it. It's often completely deserted.

- **HARBOUR** in the province is Halifax Harbour, which is about 8 km long. At its mouth it's about 2 km wide, with a narrow channel that leads to a huge inner harbour. This also makes Halifax Harbour the second largest in the world after Sydney, Australia, and, at a depth of 18 meters at low tide, one of the deepest harbours in the world, and the harbour with the largest water volume in the world.

3. **Cape George**. Cape George, on the Bras d'Or Lakes, is not to be confused with the other Cape George near Antigonish. (Why did our ancestors do this?) A double tombolo, Cape George is linked to the adjoining land by two beaches with a barachois lagoon trapped between them. The twin gravel beaches separate the warm salty water of the Lakes from the warm fresh water of the barachois. Cruising in Silversark, I like to go ashore with a bar of soap, and use the lagoon as a vast bathtub.

4. **Marble Mountain**. Also on the Bras d'Or Lakes, Marble Mountain is unique: a beach of white marble fragments which drops steeply into crystal-clear water at the base of high cliffs where limestone once was quarried. Cruising yachts from all over the world stop here, and the offshore waters are crowded with wooded islands which can easily be reached with a kayak or an inflatable. North America's most easterly and northerly vineyard is nearby — not, alas, open to the public, but a testimony to the relative mildness of the summer climate.

5. **Pondville Beach**. On the eastern shore of Isle Madame, Pondville Beach is my home beach, a complete beach system stretching seven miles between the tree-line and the deep water. A little stream nourishes it with sediments from the middle of the island, and the tiny reed-rimmed estuary makes a children's swimming hole. A small lagoon behind the low dunes sustains muskrats and water birds. Most of the beach is sandy, but in one spot big cobbles roll in the surf, clacking and rattling in the backwash.

Did you know...

OFFSHORE

The sea, or offshore, is a defining characteristic of Nova Scotia. With the adoption of the 200-mile limit in 1977, the offshore segment of the province — an area of almost 400,000 square km — is larger than the land portion by a magnitude of four. The straits, seas and, of course, the Atlantic Ocean are more than just geological descriptors, they are an important influence on how Nova Scotians see themselves and how many people outside the province view them.

CONTINENTAL SHELF AND SLOPE

Beyond Nova Scotia's coastline lies an underwater continental shelf that extends like a submerged coastal plain from 125 to 230 km seaward. The average depth is 90 m, with deeper basins and troughs that descend more than 200 m.

Bordering the shelf are the deeper ocean waters of the continental slope that quickly descend to depths of over three kilometers. The major offshore areas making up the continental shelf are the Northumberland Strait, southeastern Gulf of St. Lawrence, Sydney Bight, Scotian Shelf, Georges Bank, Gulf of Maine, and the Bay of Fundy. A major feature of the shelf is a series of shallow banks that culminate at Sable Island, a 42 kilometer-long spit of land rising just 26 m above sea level.

Did you know...

Bay of Fundy

The way author Esther Shephard tells it in her version of the old legend, it was the mythical giant Paul Bunyan who first caused the great tides to run in the Bay of Fundy — the infant Paul Bunyan at that!

"Paul was asleep in his cradle when they went to get him," she wrote, "and they had to send for the British navy and it took seven hours of bombardin' to wake him up. And when Paul stepped out of his cradle it made such a swell it caused a 75-foot tide in the Bay of Fundy and several villages was swept away and seven of the invincible English warships was sunk to the bottom of the sea."

The great cataclysm passed and Paul moved on, but, Shephard wrote, "the tides in the Bay of Fundy is just as high as they ever was."

Indeed, the tides of the Bay of Fundy are the largest in the world, rising some 16 meters, or the equivalent of a four-storey building. Twice a day, 200 billion tonnes of water enter and leave the Bay of Fundy, an amount equal to all the rivers on Earth.

The tidal exchange of the Bay of Fundy means the waters stretching as far as Georges Bank get a twice-daily vertical mixing, making the waters nutritionally rich and the fishing grounds enormously productive. (Unfortunately for some parts of southwestern Nova Scotia, it also makes it the fog capital of the province.)

The Bay of Fundy is in part responsible for sustaining a large herring stock off southwestern Nova Scotia. Lobster and scallop fisheries also benefit from the Fundy tides and these fisheries are the most important industry in many of the communities that dot the shoreline.

Weather

Predicting the weather in Nova Scotia is not for the faint of heart. Mark Twain could very easily have been talking about Nova Scotia when he said if you don't like the weather, just wait a minute. Winds moving eastward from the interior of the continent combined with the mixing of two major ocean currents — the Labrador Current, bringing the cold waters of the North Atlantic, and the Gulf Stream, bringing warm waters from the Gulf of Mexico — make it a witch's brew that confounds even the best of meteorologists.

What this all means is that as a result of cool waters, springtime weather is marked by similarly cool winds, often extending the spring season into June. The upside is that late springs develop into late autumns, with the now-warmer waters giving Nova Scotians an extra boost before Old Man Winter sets in.

TEMPERATURES
- Spring: 2° to 9° C
- Summer: 16° to 24° C
- Autumn: 12° to 18° C
- Winter: -3° to -6° C
- Coldest month of the year: February
- Warmest month of the year: July

AND THE WINNER IS . . .

- **Record high:** August 19, 1935 in Collegeville, Guysborough County: 38.3° C
- **Record low:** January 31, 1921 in Upper Stewiacke: -41.1° C
- **Windiest day:** January 18, 1990 when the maximum hourly speed reached 135 km in Halifax
- **Rainiest day:** August 15, 1971 when 218.2 mm of rain was recorded at Halifax Stanfield International Airport
- **Snowiest day:** February 19, 2004 in Halifax: 95 cm

SUNSHINE

Nova Scotia is Canada's eighth sunniest province. Each year, Nova Scotians can expect to see the sun on an average of 289 days per year, which is considerably more than Nunavut, who see the sun on only 226 days per year but less than Alberta, who see 312 sunny days each year.

RAIN

- Average number of rainy days per year: 170
- Average annual rainfall amount: 1,178 millimeters

GROWING SEASON

- Growing season: May to September
- Number of frost-free days per year in Nova Scotia: 120
- In the farmlands of the Annapolis Valley: 140
- Highlands of Cape Breton Island: 100

Did you know...

that the area of Browns Bank, 60 km south of Cape Sable, is visited by about 200 northern right whales each year?

SNOW

- Percentage of annual precipitation that falls as snow: 15
- Average number of days per year there is snow on the ground somewhere in Nova Scotia: 110
- Average amount of snow that falls each year along the coast: 150 cm
- Inland: 250 cm
- In northern Cape Breton: 300 cm

Bring it Juan

The most destructive storm in Nova Scotia's history occurred on September 29, 2003, a Category 2 hurricane named Juan. Having quietly crept up the eastern seaboard from its birthplace in Bermuda, this storm landed at about midnight, walloping Nova Scotia and carving a path of destruction through Halifax and Truro.

With maximum sustained winds of 151 km/h, and maximum winds gusts of 176 km/h, literally millions of trees in the province were uprooted. That included over 70 percent - 55,000 - of the trees in Halifax's scenic Point Pleasant Park. The seas surged about two meters along the coastline, while the maximum wave height recorded during the storm reached almost 20 m.

Between 800,000 to 900,000 residents of Nova Scotia and Prince Edward Island lost power at some point during the storm, and it took Nova Scotia Power over two weeks to restore power to all its customers. In total, Juan caused over $200 million worth of damage to the province in a period of just three hours. Eight people were killed as a result of the storm.

PASS THE SHOVEL

Nova Scotia is the fifth snowiest province or territory, with an annual average of 259 cm of snow. Newfoundland and Labrador is the snowiest province with 452 cm and Alberta receives the least amount of snow with 140 cm. Nova Scotia also has the fifth snowiest spring and the least snowy fall.

Nova Scotia is tenth in Canada when it comes to snow days with an average of 62 each year, behind Quebec which gets 109 and dead last when it comes to snowfall as a percentage of precipitation. The province sits at 20 percent compared to Nunavut with 62 percent. Despite having the mildest winter, Nova Scotia still has 14 blowing snow days each year.

Source: Environment Canada

WHITE CHRISTMAS

The chances of having a white Christmas in Nova Scotia vary, depending on where you are celebrating the holiday. Halifax has a 59 percent chance of a white Christmas, while there is a 40 percent chance along the Atlantic Coast of the province. The province has a 24 percent chance of a 'perfect' Christmas, which is defined as having at least 2 cm of snow on the ground and snow in the air. The greatest snowfall recorded on Christmas Day in Halifax was 17.7 cm in 2000.

Source: Meteorological Service of Canada

WINDS

- Spring and summer winds typically blow from south or southwest at speeds of 10 to 15 km/h.
- Autumn and winter winds typically blow from west and northwest at speeds of 20 to 25 km/h.

LES SUETES

Along the western shores of Cape Breton, especially around Cheticamp and Grand Etang, there's a local wind phenomenon known as les suetes. These sudden windstorms are well known in the area for the wide destruction they can cause. They occur when warm air off the ocean collides with the cold air of the Cape Breton Highlands. The air swirls together and descends eastward down the mountains, gathering speed as it goes. The strongest suete ever recorded happened on March 13, 1993, blowing at 233 km/hour.

Bring it Juan Part II

With the memories of Hurricane Juan still fresh in folks' minds, the fiercest winter storm ever to strike Nova Scotia occurred the following winter, on February 18th and 19th, 2004. Snowfall records were shattered. Winds reaching near record levels shut down the province for days afterward.

- Amount of snow that fell across Nova Scotia: 40 to 100 cm
- Amount that typically accumulated per hour during the storm: 7 cm
- Amount that typically accumulates per hour during a normal winter storm in Nova Scotia: 2 to 3 cm
- Maximum wind gusts recorded during the storm: 124 km/hr
- Amount of snow that fell in Halifax and Dartmouth: 95.5 cm
- Amount of snow that fell in Sydney: 40.8 cm
- Amount of snow that fell in Yarmouth: 82.6 cm

HARNESSING THE WIND

Nova Scotia's first wind powered electrical generating facility opened in May 2005 at Pubnico Point and now has 41 wind turbines which stretch from Yarmouth County to Inverness County. The turbines generate 60 megawatts of power and account for 2.5 percent of Nova Scotia's energy needs or enough to power 20,000 homes. Nova Scotia Power Inc. currently has contracts with several different wind power companies with the potential to generate 100 mw of power.

Source: Nova Scotia Power Inc.

Take 5 PETER COADE'S
FIVE THINGS YOU DIDN'T KNOW ABOUT NOVA SCOTIA WEATHER

Peter Coade has been studying weather since joining the federal government's weather service in 1962. He has worked at centers in Nova Scotia, Newfoundland (Goose Bay) and Ontario. Immediately prior to 'returning home' to Halifax and becoming a familiar face to viewers of ATV/ASN in Atlantic Canada, Coade was the manager of the Toronto Weather Office. While in Toronto, he was also the staff meteorologist for CFRB radio station, working alongside such personalities as the late Gordon Sinclair and Betty Kennedy (of Front Page Challenge fame) and was the Air Committee meteorologist for the Canadian International Air Show (CIAS/CNE). In September 2007, Coade made the move to CBC's *News at Six* as their weathercaster.

1. Wind is a significant factor on the plateau of the Cape Breton Highlands, and also on the west coast (Inverness County) where winds from the southeast — locally called les suetes — typically reach hurricane force, gusting up to 200 kilometers per hour. High southeast winds gain speed over the open plateau and tumble down onto the western coast in turbulent gusts, buffeting local communities.

FOG

The number of potentially sunny days in the province each year is decreased by fifty percent because of fog.

- Longest stretch of fog ever recorded was 85 days in the summer of 1967 in the town of Yarmouth.
- Number of days Yarmouth was without fog that summer: 7

2. The highest tides on Earth occur in the Minas Basin, the eastern extremity of the Bay of Fundy, where the average tide range is 12 meters and can reach 17 meters when the various factors affecting the tides are in phase.

3. Nova Scotia is almost an island, with no point in the province more than 60 km from the water. In the late spring and early summer, warm southerly breezes produce extensive fog along the Atlantic coast, but that short drive to the other side of the province reveals warmth and sunshine. It is the effect of these same southerly breezes blowing in off the cold North Atlantic that inhibit the production of severe thunderstorms and tornadoes — a rarity in the province.

4. Although Nova Scotia has what is termed a "maritime climate", it is greatly modified in certain months of the year to possess a "continental climate. As a result, temperature extremes on record vary from near −40°C in the depths of winter to near +40°C in the summer months.

5. According to the publication, *The Climate of Canada*, Nova Scotia is called 'the stormiest province.'

Take 5 — TOP FIVE FOGGIEST PLACES
IN NOVA SCOTIA

1. **Sable Island:** 152 days per year
2. **Halifax:** 122 days
3. **Yarmouth:** 118 days
4. **Canso:** 115 days
5. **Dartmouth:** 101 days

CAN YOU SAY CYCLONE?

A disastrous tropical cyclone that struck Cape Breton Island in 1873 led to the establishment of a Canadian storm warning system. Residents were caught so unprepared for the storm that over 500 lives were lost, 1,200 vessels sank, and 900 buildings were damaged or leveled. At the time, losses were estimated at $3.5 million, equivalent to about $70 million today. The telegraph service at the time had momentarily been interrupted, preventing storm warnings from Toronto getting to Halifax, helping to convince officials of the need to establish a separate storm warning system for Canada.

Did you know...

that there are over 150 lighthouses in Nova Scotia, which give ships at sea a beacon of light through the fog and the dark of the night? At one time they were staffed by lighthouse keepers, but today they are all automated.

Take 5 TOP FIVE MOST DESTRUCTIVE HURRICANES IN NOVA SCOTIA

1. **Hurricane Juan** - 2003
2. **Hurricane Edna** - 1954
3. **Hurricane Carol** - 1953
4. **Great Atlantic Hurricane** - 1944
5. **Portland Gale** - 1898

NOR'EASTER

- Typical Nor'easter wind speed: 150 km/h
- Typical peak wave heights: 14 m
- Amount of snow a Nor'easter typically brings: 25 cm

HURRICANES AND TROPICAL STORMS

- Average number that affect Atlantic Canada each year: 3 or 4
- Last year in which a Category 4 or 5 hurricane struck Nova Scotia: 1851
- Number of Category 2 hurricanes that have struck Nova Scotia in the past 110 years: 2

Did you know...

that the most winter lightning in Canada occurs in an area just south of Sable Island in the Atlantic Ocean? Here, the cold air from the Arctic collides with the warm air of the Gulf of Mexico, creating ideal conditions for thunderstorms and lightning.

Did you know...

that the earliest storm ever recorded in Nova Scotia was the Great Hurricane of August 1635 that hit the coast of Massachusetts on its northward track, wrecking ships arriving with new colonists and destroying thousands of huge trees? It then passed through Nova Scotia near Cape Sable.

TORNADOES

Tornadoes are extremely rare in Nova Scotia. The last major one reported was in Liverpool on January 30, 1954, which was accompanied by heavy hail and lightning.

EARTHQUAKES

Earthquakes in Nova Scotia are rare, and mostly occur off the coast. Since 1954, 72 minor earthquakes have been recorded on the ocean floor, registering between 1.6 and 3.8 on the Richter scale.

The only earthquake to result in any major damage in Nova Scotia occurred off the coast of Newfoundland in 1929, which generated a

Did you know...

that the number of trees lost in Nova Scotia and Prince Edward Island as a result of Hurricane Juan totaled over 100 million?

Did you know...

that strange weather isn't the only weird thing that happens in the sky over Nova Scotia? According to the researchers at the University of Manitoba, there were 23 reported sightings of UFOs in the skies over Nova Scotia during 2004.

tidal wave that struck Cape Breton Island. Though spared the widespread coastal devastation suffered by Newfoundland, one Cape Bretoner was killed and minor damage was done to the shoreline and seaside homes.

Perhaps the most famous earthquake to have ever been felt in Nova Scotia was the great Lisbon earthquake of 1755, off the coast of Portugal, which caused a few minor tremors along the Nova Scotia shoreline.

Source: Geological Survey of Canada

Weblinks

Weather Winners
www.on.ec.gc.ca/weather/winners/intro-e.html
Find out how cities across Canada rank in 72 different weather categories at the Environment Canada website.

Hurricane Juan 2003 Special Report
www.ns.ec.gc.ca/weather/hurricane/juan/
Read Environment Canada's special report on Nova Scotia's most destructive hurricane.

Nova Scotia Weather Forecast
www.theweathernetwork.com/weather/cancitiesns_en
Find out what the weather is going to be like in your city or town.

Crime and Punishment

CRIME LINE

1749: First murder in Halifax, followed by Canada's first ever trial under British Law.

1835: Joseph Howe publishes his famous letter and is charged with Libel. After defending himself, Howe is acquitted.

1844: The mutinous, murderous crew of the Saladin are hanged publicly.

1923: J.B. McLachlan is charged with sedition and sentenced to two years.

1937: In Nova Scotia's last execution, Everett Farmer is hanged for murder.

1964: Aubrey Lutz confesses to Kentville RCMP members that he has shot four people. Three of the four are killed.

1971: Donald Marshall Jr. is wrongly accused of murder.

1989: 19-year-old Kimberly McAndrew is seen leaving her workplace at Canadian Tire and is never heard from again.

1990: The province officially apologizes to Donald Marshall Jr.

1990: Largest hashish seizure in Canadian history goes down in Ragged Harbour, NS.

1992: Three people are killed and a fourth injured after a botched robbery in Sydney River's McDonald's restaurant. Three men are handed life sentences for the murders.

1992: Crime Stoppers program is initiated in the province.

1998: Gail Stone and her common-law husband Richard Marriott are gunned down at their Halifax home. Their killer has never been found.

2002: Clayton Johnson, wrongfully convicted for the 1993 murder of his wife, has his conviction overturned and is freed.

2004: Nova Scotia Supreme Court celebrates its 250th birthday.

They Said It

"A hanging day . . . brings the worst of Halifax to the market place. They press against the gallows, their eyes eager. A fiendish festivity marks the occasion. They cheer at the launching and persist in mocking the hanged-man until his final gasp."
— **The fictional character "Fetch," Robert E. Kroll (ed).**
Intimate Fragments: An Irreverent Chronicle of Early Halifax.

Fury of a Madman

"I've done a terrible thing. I shot four people." This was the chilling confession of Aubrey Lutz, made to officers at the Kentville, N.S. RCMP detachment on February 12th, 1964. Lutz had recently married 18-year-old Rosalie Pudsey.

Rosalie and Aubrey's marriage began to sour, and fearing for her safety, Rosalie took the couples' newborn baby, Kimberly, to live with her parents and two sisters. Rosalie's move enraged Aubrey, and on that fateful day he loaded his gun and went to confront his wife and her family. Aubrey met and killed Rosalie's mother first. When Rosalie's younger sister Audrey sought refuge in the bathroom, Aubrey fired through the door, instantly killing the 15-year-old. On hearing the commotion, Rosalie Lutz climbed the stairs from the basement and placed baby Kimberly on the living room couch. When she confronted her husband, he fired, striking her in the shoulder.

Just as Aubrey was about to make his escape, Arthur Pudsey returned home to the awful scene. For the fourth time Aubrey fired his gun, this time killing his father-in-law. Aubrey grabbed his unharmed baby and travelled to Kentville where he confessed to police. Rosalie Lutz and her nine-year old sister, who had been at school, were the sole surviving members of their family.

Deemed unfit to stand trial, Lutz was sent to the Nova Scotia Hospital. For almost fifteen years he remained a volatile, dangerous man who was heavily medicated and received almost 500 shock treatments.

In the late 1970s and 1980s, however, Lutz's demeanor improved and he was classified a voluntary patient, free to check himself out. On December 27th, 1990, the murderer of three left the Nova Scotia Hospital a free man and returned to his Annapolis Valley home. Horrified, Rosalie called police. Lutz was again arrested, charged with three counts of murder and prepared for trial.

In March 1991, the courts made a familiar ruling — Lutz was deemed unfit for trial, and remanded into the custody of the Nova Scotia Hospital, where he remains. Amazingly, Rosalie has forgiven Aubrey: "I believe everyone should leave him alone. I have forgiven my husband for what he has done."

2004: Theresa McEvoy is killed when a stolen car, driven by a delinquent teen, runs a stop sign and crashes into her car. The death sparks a major wake-up call to the government in relation to troubled teens and youth crime.

2005: Nova Scotians are shocked when two affable young men from the peaceful community of Glen Haven are discovered murdered. 25-year-old Michael Joseph Mitchelmore is charged with first-degree murder shortly thereafter.

2005: Danny DiBenedetto is shot and killed in his Dartmouth home. Three masked men are seen fleeing the area but are never caught. DiBenedetto leaves behind a wife and young son.

2007: On New Years Eve, police make the shocking discovery of 20-year-old Jennifer Horne's lifeless body in a closet, wrapped in a carpet. She had been assaulted, tortured, and then brutally murdered. Desmond Maguire, 37, and Ashley Haley, 20, are charged with her murder.

CRIME BY THE NUMBERS (2006)
- 75,393 criminal code incidents
- 16 homicides
- 8,585 assaults

They Said It

"We are all capable of murder ... People have their breaking points. ... I really do think that when it comes to murder, we're all brothers and sisters, and we could all be murderers in the right circumstances."
— **Donald Clairmont, director of the Atlantic Institute of Criminology**

- 790 robberies
- 2,460 motor vehicle theft
- 6,865 break and enters
- 804 sexual assaults
- 2,040 drug violations
- 2,379 cases of impaired driving
- 14,936 mischief cases

Source: Stats Can

Murderous Mutinies

In May of 1844, the ship Saladin ran aground on Nova Scotia's eastern shore. Claims made from the small crew of six was that the captain and other crew members had died at sea, which raised immediate suspicions. The crew was placed under arrest, and charged with killing their captain and five crewmates.

As confessions were elicited, a grizzly story of mutiny and murder took shape. The ringleader, George Fielding (this former captain had been in prison prior to the journey, but made a deal with authorities to work the trip for free passage for himself and his 14-year-old son), had convinced four crewmen to help him carry out his dastardly deed. On April 14, 1844, they used axes and other tools on board to kill the captain and five mates. When his compatriots learned of Fielding's plans to sweeten his own share of the loot through further killings, they turned on him, throwing him and his son overboard.

After only 15 minutes of deliberation, the jury returned guilty verdicts in three cases. Two of the men, tried separately, were acquitted. The convicted pirates were hanged on July 30, 1844. Hundreds of Haligonians brought their families to witness the event on the South Common, the site today of the Victoria General Hospital.

MURDER

According to Donald Clairmont, director of the Atlantic Institute of Criminology at Dalhousie University, people kill for three reasons: passion, profit, or inexplicably, for no apparent reason.

In 2006, there were 16 homicides in Nova Scotia, 2.6 percent of the total 605 homicides reported to police in Canada in 2006. The rate of homicide per 100,000 of the Nova Scotian population is 1.71, lower than the national rate of 1.85.

STOLEN CARS

As of 2006, the rate of motor vehicle theft in Nova Scotia was 263.3 for each 100,000 people, making it the highest in Atlantic Canada. The highest rate is in Manitoba, with 1,375.7. The lowest is in Prince Edward Island where the rate is 114.8. The national rate stands at 487.2.

IMPAIRED DRIVING

As of 2006, Nova Scotia's impaired driving offences rate was 254.6 per 100,000 people, making it the second highest in Atlantic Canada behind Prince Edward Island. The North West Territories is the overall highest at a staggering 1,168.2 per 100,000. Canada's overall impaired driving rate sits at 227.9.

FINE, THEN

The total fine often depends on whether it is a first, second or third offence.
• Speeding, 10-30 km over: $150 / $300 / $600

They Said It

"The business of one half of the town is to sell rum, and the other half to drink it."
— **Rev. Dr. Ezra Stiles, President of Yale College, referring to Halifax.**

- Speeding, 31 km or more over: $250 / $500 / $1,000
- Speeding in a school zone: $150 / $300 / $600
- Driving with a suspended or revoked license: $500 / $1,000 / $2,000
- Failure to yield to a pedestrian in a crosswalk: $250 / $500 / $1,000
- Failure to stop at the scene of an accident: $250 / $500 / $1,000
- Parking in a disabled parking spot: $100 / $200 / $400
- Failure to wear a helmet on a motorcycle: $100 / $200 / $400
- Driving without a license: $150 / $300 / $600
- Failure to wear a seatbelt: $50 / $100 / $200
- Failure to stop at a stop sign: $50 / $100 / $200
- Parking Violations: $5 / $10

Source: Service Nova Scotia

CANADA'S FIRST TRIAL FOR MURDER

Peter Cartcel has the dubious distinction of being the first Halifax murderer charged and tried for his crime. On August 26th, 1749, Cartcel fatally stabbed Abraham Goodsides as the two fought on the streets of the infant city. Because Nova Scotia had no court system, the murder required Gov. Edward Cornwallis to take immediate action.

Empowered to establish courts for the fledging city, Cornwallis named himself and six councillors to the city's first court. On the 31st of August, Cartcel appeared without a lawyer before the hastily established court for Canada's first ever trial under British law. After hearing four witnesses, the court deliberated for just half an hour before they found the defendant guilty. Two days later, Cartcel was hanged.

They Said It

"*We're talking about massive amounts. Even today, we still don't have any idea how much is getting through. We do know, though, that the seizures we do make are only a small portion of the total picture.*"

— **Gary Grant, RCMP, on drug smuggling in Nova Scotia**

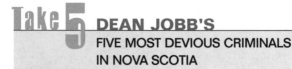

Take 5 DEAN JOBB'S
FIVE MOST DEVIOUS CRIMINALS
IN NOVA SCOTIA

Dean Jobb hunted down Nova Scotia's most intriguing criminals for three books of true-crime stories, including *Shades of Justice: Seven Nova Scotia Murder Cases*, winner of the Evelyn Richardson award for best non-fiction work by a Nova Scotia writer. He is also the author of *The Acadians: A Peoples Story of Exile and Triumph* and *Calculated Risk: Greed, Politics and the Westray Tragedy*. A former reporter, editor and columnist for the *Halifax Herald*, Dean is an assistant professor of journalism at the University of King's College in Halifax. He lives in Wolfville.

1. **Lt.-Colonel Charles Lawrence:** Nova Scotia's acting governor in 1755, Lawrence was the driving force behind the brutal expulsion of 10,000 Acadian men, women and children from their homeland and their dispersal to the American Colonies, England and France. At least 5,000 deportees died of disease and hunger or drowned in shipwrecks in an act of genocide and ethnic cleansing that ranks Lawrence among the world's most ruthless criminals.

2. **The Saladin Pirates:** They are hardly household names, but Charles Anderson, John Hazelton, George Jones and William Travaskiss committed one of the bloodiest mutinies of the Age of Sail. On a voyage from South America to England in 1844, they rose up against the captain of the cargo ship Saladin and later tossed the ringleader of the mutiny overboard. A shocking tale of the murder of eight men emerged after the ship ran aground on the Eastern Shore. The four were tried, convicted, and publicly hanged on the Halifax Commons.

3. **Samuel Herbert Dougal:** When Dougal, a retired soldier, was convicted of murdering a wealthy heiress in Britain in 1903, Scotland Yard detectives started asking questions about the sudden deaths of

two Halifax women almost two decades earlier. Dougal, a sergeant in the Royal Engineers, was stationed in Halifax in June 1885 when his first wife, Lovenia, died. He remarried Mary Boyd six weeks later but she died that October. Bad luck? Coincidence? The authorities could not rule out the possibility that Dougal had been a serial killer who preyed on women.

4. **Jack Randell:** His motto was "Once a scrapper, always a scrapper," and Newfoundland-born skipper Randell was a scrapper. In March 1929, he was at the wheel of the Lunenburg-based rumrunner I'm Alone, trying to land a load of illegal booze in Louisiana, when a U.S. Coast Guard cutter chased his schooner deep into international waters. The cutter opened fire, sending the I'm Alone to the bottom, killing one of Randell's crewmen and sparking a diplomatic row between Canada and the U.S. The Americans later apologized for the breach of international law and compensated Randell for the loss of his boat.

5. **James Forman:** The first cashier of the Bank of Nova Scotia almost turned out to be its last. In 1870, a junior clerk stumbled upon a shortfall in the accounts of the bank, which was founded in Halifax in 1835. It turned out to be the tip of an iceberg — $320,000 was missing, embezzled over the previous 25 years to finance Forman's lavish lifestyle, which included a mansion in the city's fashionable south end. As the size of the fraud became apparent, Forman fled to London to escape prosecution. He died there the following year. The bank, nearly ruined by the loss and the blow to public confidence, soldiered on to become one of Canada's leading financial institutions.

Take 5 — TOP FIVE COMMUNITIES WITH THE MOST POLICE (PER CAPITA)

1. Annapolis Royal
2. Kentville
3. Bridgewater
4. Amherst
5. Trenton

NO BETTER WAY TO SPEND A SATURDAY WITH THE KIDDIES

Nova Scotians found guilty of capital crimes in the 18th, 19th and even the early 20th centuries faced death by hanging. In 1785 alone, 12 people were hanged - one of those charged with stealing potatoes! Entertainment-starved Haligonians eagerly staked out the best vantage point from which to view hangings, which were often held in public spots such as the market or on the Commons.

GAOL OF GEORGE'S ISLAND

Time in jail at George's Island off the Halifax shore was no island retreat. Like most prisons of the day, Her Majesty's Georges Island Gaol of the 1700s and 1800s was the wretched home of rats and rogues and their communicable maladies. For more than a century, errant military men — traitors, mutineers and deserters, as well as unfortunate civilians — were imprisoned on the island while they awaited their fates — exile, flogging, or death by hanging.

They Said It

"One of the most dangerous times for a woman (and her children) is when she leaves."
— Former chairwoman of the NS Advisory Council on the Status of Women, Patricia Doyle Bedwell

OUTLAWING LIQUOR

In the late 19th and early 20th centuries, the use and sale of alcohol was a political and social hot potato. Following a crusade that began in the early nineteenth century, pro-temperance Nova Scotians got their wish when Canada passed the 1878 Canada Temperance Act legislation that allowed all communities to vote on whether or not

McDonald's Murders

In the early pre-dawn morning of May 7th, 1992, three young Sydney-area men arrived at the city's McDonald's restaurant intending to commit robbery. Derek Wood, Darren Muise and Freeman MacNeil were sure that the restaurant's safe contained as much as $200,000.

The robbery turned deadly when the three encountered the four staff members on the midnight shift. Armed with knives, a .22 caliber pistol and a shovel, the three robbers brutally murdered Donna Warren, Neil Borroughs and Jimmy Fagan, and left Arlene MacNeil badly wounded and near death.

The horrific crime stunned and outraged the small city, and indeed the whole nation, as national media descended on Sydney. The perpetrators denied their involvement but evidence against them mounted, and by the middle of May all had confessed their crime.

They were variously charged with murder, robbery and the unlawful confinement of Donna Warren, who had been forced to open the safe before she, like the others, was shot in the head. Harsh punishment was meted out to the murderers. Darren Muise was sentenced to life in prison without parole for twenty years and Freeman MacNeil got life in prison with no parole for twenty-five years. Derek Wood was sentenced to two life terms in jail, and ten years for robbery and unlawful confinement.

they would become 'dry.'

Most Nova Scotian municipalities - one exception being Halifax - voted to outlaw drinking. With the Temperance Act of 1910, Nova Scotians were legally allowed to buy alcohol only for "medicinal, sacramental, art, trade and manufacturing purposes." Again, Halifax was the exception; there, people continued to drink, entitled by law.

In 1916, Nova Scotia abandoned the local option approach to prohibition and went stone dry. Alcohol consumption was banned across the province, even in Halifax. For the next 14 years, Nova Scotians could not legally have a drink.

(RUM) RUNNING FROM THE LAW

Out of prohibition sprung a new, lucrative and illegal rum trade. Former temperance inspector enforcement officer and New Glasgow native Clifford Rose recalls that his own sleepy Nova Scotia hamlet contained illegal rum dives that were "thick as bees."

One of the most colourful characters in Rose's memoirs is Delores N., the feisty proprietor of a local watering hole and a woman with an "obscene and profane tongue," a disabled husband and several children to raise.

In one raid on Delores' establishment, the businesswoman acquainted the back of Rose's head with a liquor bottle. Recognizing the pervasiveness of the illegal industry, the financial rewards that drove Nova Scotians like Delores to embrace it, and the utter corruption of so-called enforcement officials, a cynical Rose celebrated the 1929 defeat of prohibition in his province.

Did you know...

that Nova Scotia has 87 courtrooms?

SMUGGLER'S PARADISE

Nova Scotia is still a haven for smuggling illicit substances, thanks to its sheltered coves and inlets and its isolated, unguarded coastline. In the late 1970s, heightened coastal protection in the United States, coupled with its geography, made Nova Scotia a favoured drop-off spot for drug smugglers. While the entire South Shore has seen a rapid rise in smuggling activity over the past three decades, the remote coasts of Queens and Shelburne counties have emerged as the biggest 'pipelines' for illegal drug transactions.

In the 1970s, the Coastal Watch Program was initiated at RCMP request. Nova Scotians living near the coast are asked to report suspi-

End of an Era

Everett Farmer, a Nova Scotian labourer charged with murdering his brother-in-law, was the last person to be hanged in the province. As a poor, black, Shelburne County man, Farmer had access to legal counsel of dubious quality. Farmer insisted that his crime had been one of self-defense, but without adequate representation it was hard for him to make his case.

A lawyer was not assigned to his defense until just one week before the opening of his September 1937 trial. As the first capital case to be heard in Shelburne County for a century, the Farmer trial became a media circus.

Juried by twelve white men, the trial lasted just two days and ended in a murder conviction. Everett Farmer was sentenced to die. According to a newspaper account, at 5 a.m. on December 15th, Farmer climbed the stairs of the hanging scaffold "with the same coolness that [had] characterized him since he [had] been in jail." As the hood was placed over his head, and as his spiritual advisor recited scripture, Farmer uttered his last words before the trap was sprung; "Good-bye, boys."

cious offshore activities. RCMP estimates suggest that 10 percent of the cocaine and 50 percent of the cannabis imported into Canada arrives by water, and a good deal of this comes via Nova Scotia's South Shore.

On May 27th, 1990, the largest seizure of hashish in Canadian history went down in Ragged Harbour, Nova Scotia. Thanks to reports

Eleven Lost Years

On May 28th, 1971, sixteen-year-old Donald Marshall Jr. was walking through a Sydney park when he met up with Sandy Seale, another youth from Sydney. The two teenagers then encountered Roy Ebsary, described as an "eccentric old man with a fetish for knives." Without warning, Ebsary brutally and fatally stabbed Seale.

Police arrested and charged Marshall, a Mi'kmaq from Membertou, with Seale's death, and in November 1971 Marshall was sentenced to life in prison. For 11 years Marshall was incarcerated; for 11 years he maintained his innocence. In 1982, Marshall was released on bail as then Justice Minister, Jean Chrétien, referred the case to the Nova Scotia Supreme Court for rehearing.

In 1983, Donald Marshall Jr. was acquitted of all charges, but in a strange outcome the police who had wrongly charged him were absolved of all wrongdoing. In a now infamous statement, Chrétien reasoned that any miscarriage of justice was "more apparent than real." Roy Ebsary was eventually convicted of manslaughter in the death of Seale. For eleven lost years of his life, Donald Marshall accepted a lump sum payment of $270,000 from the Nova Scotia government, but was required to pay his own legal bills.

furnished by a local lobster fisherman, police were tipped off to a smuggling operation of 25 tonnes of hashish, with an estimated street value of more than $400 million.

In February 1994, Nova Scotian authorities made another huge bust off the rocky shore of Nova Scotia. Two years of RCMP investigations were rewarded with a massive drug seizure in Shelburne. The vessel, Lady Teri-Anne, was weighed down with 5,419 kilograms of cocaine, worth $1 billion.

FAKIN' IT
In 2006, there were 2,312 counterfeit bank notes passed and seized by police in Nova Scotia — accounting for about one percent of the 322,486 phony bills that were passed and seized nationwide. Nationally, seized counterfeit notes had a face value of $6,659,048.
Source: RCMP

CORRECTIONAL FACILITIES
There are seven prisons in Nova Scotia; five for adults (in Amherst, Dartmouth, Antigonish, Yarmouth and Sydney) and two for youth (in Waterville and Glace Bay). The Southwest Nova Scotia Correctional Facility in Yarmouth opened in 2003 as a 38-bed direct supervision facility. The Central Nova Scotia Correctional Facility was built in 2001. The Nova Scotia Youth Centre in Waterville opened in 1988 and accommodates 120 youth offenders. The Cape Breton Young Offender Detention Centre is used mainly as a short term holding centre for youth before appearing in court and being transferred to Waterville if needed.

Did you know...

that 25 percent of callers to Nova Scotia Crime Stoppers' tip line are criminals themselves?

TAKING A BITE OUT OF CRIME

Nova Scotia's Crime Stoppers have been helping solve crimes since 1987. In 2007, they . . .

- Received 3,470 tips
- Arrested 14 fugitives
- Cleared 132 cases
- Recovered $188,711 worth of property
- Seized over $1.3 million worth of illegal drugs
- Paid out $8,900 in awards

Source: Nova Scotia Crime Stoppers

Weblinks

Halifax Regional Police
www.halifax.ca/police/index.asp
History, services, divisions, family programs, unsolved crimes and statistics, and details of their Netwatch program.

Royal Canadian Mounted Police
www.rcmp-grc.gc.ca/index_e.htm
This division of the RCMP serves Nova Scotia with seven detachments — links to each are found here along with a whole bunch of general information about the force.

Nova Scotia Department of Justice
www.gov.ns.ca/Just/Divisions/Related_Agencies/polcomm.asp
A website that tells you the most popular justice-related links and featured items of interest. Maybe you can even earn $50,000 by helping the police solve a major unsolved crime.

Culture

Despite having a population under one million, Nova Scotia boasts a rich and diverse cultural sector. It contributes approximately $745 million to the province's GDP each year, and almost 19,000 jobs are connected to the province's culture industry.

In 2006/07 Nova Scotia received a total of $4.2 million, or an average of $1,170 per artist, in funding from the Canadian Council for the Arts. Musicians received the largest share with $928,000, followed by artists involved in the theatre with $814,950 and visual artists with $737,045.

Sixty-eight percent of the funding went to artists in Halifax, while Dartmouth's artists saw 5.9 percent, and artists in Windsor received 3.6 percent. Nova Scotia receives more funding than any other Atlantic Canadian province - almost doubling what New Brunswick gets. But Atlantic Canada receives little compared to other provinces; in 2006/07 Ontario received almost $52 million.

Source: Canadian Council for the Arts

ARTISTS
- Number of artists in Nova Scotia: 3,500
- Number of artists in Canada: 131,700
- Nova Scotia's artists' average earnings: $23,500

Take 5 — FIVE MUSICIAN FAVOURITES
FROM NOVA SCOTIA

1. **Anne Murray**
2. **Sarah McLaughlin**
3. **Rita McNeil**
4. **Ashley McIsaac**
5. **Joel Plaskett**

- Gap between artists' earnings and overall workforce average: 38 percent

Source: Canadian Council for the Arts

HOUSEHOLD CULTURAL SPENDING BREAKDOWN
- Original works of art: $38
- Antiques: $10
- Recorded music and movies: $120
- Movie rentals: $95
- Going to the movies: $79
- Live performing arts: $43
- Newspapers: $106
- Magazines and periodicals: $55

Source: Stats Can

THAT'S AN ORDER
- Nova Scotian recipients of the Order of Canada: 26
- Members of the Order: 14
- Officers of the Order: 12
- Companions of the Order: 0

Did you know...

that in 2004, Nova Scotians listened to an average of 19 hours of radio programming each week?

Take 5 FIVE INTERESTING NOVA SCOTIAN MUSEUMS

1. Pier 21
2. Art Gallery of Nova Scotia
3. Maritime Museum of the Atlantic
4. Nova Scotia Museum of Natural History
5. Fortress Louisbourg

AND THE WINNER IS... RECENT NOVA SCOTIAN WINNERS OF THE GOVERNOR GENERAL'S AWARD

2007 – Don Domanski (Cape Breton): *All Our Wonder Unavenged*
2006 – William Gilkerson (Mahone Bay): *Pirate's Passage*
2001 – George Elliott Clarke (Windsor): *Execution's Poem*
1999 – Marq de Villiers (Lunenburg): *Water: The Fate of Our Most Precious Resource*

GILLER PRIZE FINALISTS FROM NOVA SCOTIA

No Nova Scotian writer has ever won the Giller Prize, however Leo McKay Jr. from Stellarton was nominated in 1995 for his collection of short stories in *Like This*.

FILM INDUSTRY

Nova Scotia is home to the fourth largest film industry in Canada behind Vancouver, Toronto and Montreal. Traditionally, made-for-TV movies have been the bread and butter of the industry, the best known of which is probably the *Jesse Stone* series starring Tom Selleck.

Several television shows have been filmed in the province including sci-fi favourite *Lexx* and popular children's program *Theodore Tugboat*. There have also been numerous feature films made here including *Titanic* with Leonardo DiCaprio, *The Scarlett Letter* starring

Winona Rider, *Two if By Sea* with Dennis Leary and Sandra Bullock and *The Shipping News* starring Kevin Spacey.

A strong Canadian dollar, along with strikes from Canada's actors union ACTRA and the US writers strike took their toll on the industry in 2007, but most people feel the province's natural scenery and experienced crew will help the industry bounce back.

Bio THOMAS H. RADDALL

Born in England in 1903, Thomas Raddall Jr. came to Canada in 1913 after his father accepted a military posting to Halifax. In the final months of WW1, his father was killed in action, essentially leaving a very young Thomas as the only male figure in the house. It was an obligation that would shape his life and writings.

As a 16-year-old, he secured a job in the Canadian Merchant Marine, staying there for three years before taking a job as a wireless operator on Sable Island. The lure of a permanent job back on the mainland brought him to Liverpool, where he worked as the accountant for pulp and paper mills on the Mersey River.

If aspiring writers complain of their lot today, they would be wise to read Raddall's autobiography to see just how difficult it was for Raddall to earn a living from the trade. Throughout his career, he never received a single writer's grant, and by the time the province recognized what they had in their midst (they offered him the Lieutenant Governorship), he and his writing belonged to the country and the world.

Raddall's early writings were short stories and were picked up by major mainstream magazines in the U.K. and the U.S., which of course had the concomitant effect of launching his career in his own country. What amazed Nova Scotians was that a writer of Raddall's ability could see in them stories worthy of telling; more amazing still was that that there was an appetite on the part of the public to read them.

Did you know...

MOVIE BUSINESS
- Number of movie theatres in Nova Scotia: 178
- Number of drive-in theatres: 3

Raddall's 1939 short story collection, *The Pied Piper of Dipper Creek*, garnered immediate popular and literary success – winning for him the Governor General's Award for Literature. A string of books followed, each centered on significant events in the history of his province.

Nova Scotia during the American Revolution was at the heart of *His Majesty's Yankees*, a book that was followed by *Roger Sudden*, an account of the fall of Louisbourg. In 1948, Raddall's non-fiction masterpiece, *Halifax: Warden of the North*, a history of Halifax, became the second of Raddall's works to win the Governor General's Award. His most highly regarded book was *The Nymph and the Lamp*, which drew upon his experiences as a radio operator on Sable Island.

In total, Raddall won three Governor General Awards in a very productive writing career. In total, he wrote more than 20 books and 32 radio and TV scripts. In 1968, Raddall retired from writing, keen to do so before his writing ability deteriorated with age.

Once asked, "Aren't you afraid of running out of material down there in a little town on the Nova Scotia coast? Why don't you move up to Toronto where there are all kinds of people and where there are all kinds of things going on?" Raddall replied, "When I run out of material where I am, I'll let you know." He never did.

Thomas Raddall died in Nova Scotia in April 1994.

Take 5 FIVE GREAT MUSIC FESTIVALS

1. **Jazz Festival**
2. **Halifax Pop Explosion**
3. **Stan Rogers Folk Festival**
4. **Lunenburg Folk Festival**
5. **Evolve**

MIKE CLATTENBURG

As mastermind of the hit television series *Trailer Park Boys*, Mike Clattenburg has created Nova Scotia's greatest cultural export in decades – some people see that as a good thing, others don't.

Clattenburg grew up in Cole Harbour and debuted on local cable access with *That Damn Cable Show* in the early 1990s. He went on to work on several CBC shows including *Street Cents* before assembling his friends Robb Wells and John Paul Tremblay to make the one hour short *One Last Shot*. A producer saw the film at the Atlantic Film Festival and one of the most foul-mouth, illegal substance-filled shows on TV was born.

In 2004, the *Trailer Park Boys* debuted in the US and in 2007, *Trailer Park Boys: The Movie* premiered in theatres. Along with *Trailer Park Boys*, Clattenburg has directed many local made-for-TV productions and music videos. He also plays drums in local rock band.

They Said It

"*I saw your band in the early days/We all understand, why you moved away/But we'll hold a grudge anyway.*"

— **Joel Plaskett from his song "Love This Town"**

Take 5 FIVE ACTORS
FROM NOVA SCOTIA

1. **Ellen Page:** *Juno, Hard Candy*
2. **Rob Wells, John Paul Tremblay and Mike Smith:** *Trailer Park Boys*
3. **Shaun Majumder:** *This Hour has 22 Minutes*
4. **Jonathan Torrens:** Host of *Jonovision*
5. **Peter North:** Adult film star

MUSIC

While Atlantic Canada's music industry has had many national and international success stories, it tends to operate in its own little corner of the country. Subsequently there are many regional stars that most Canadians living outside of the Maritimes have never heard of. Like the rest of Atlantic Canada, Nova Scotia has strong Celtic and folk music traditions.

For many years, Canadian songstress Anne Murray was probably the province's best-known international export. In the mid-1970s, Halifax rock band April Wine broke out of Canada with their album "Stand Back." Halifax's music scene exploded in the early 1990s when Moncton transplants Eric's Trip became the first Canadian band signed to influential Seattle independent record label Sub Pop.

Sloan were signed to major label DGC Records and released two records before they were dropped, broke up and reunited, becoming one of Canada's most successful rock bands of the 1990s. A signing spree swept the city which saw Jale, the Superfriendz and Joel

Did you know...

that adult contemporary and country formats account for almost half of radio ratings in Nova Scotia?

Plaskett's band Thrush Hermit sign international record contracts before the dust settled. Today, Nova Scotia's music scene encompasses almost any kind of music imaginable including rock (The Trews), folk (Old Man Luedecke), jazz (Gypsophilia), and hip hop (Classified).

GET STUFFED

To most people outside Atlantic Canada, lobster is dining in Nova Scotia and the crustacean can be eaten in pretty much any town in the province along with many other types of seafood including scallops and fish. Mediterranean food, particularly Greek and Lebanese, is popular and plentiful, particularly in Metro Halifax.

Nova Scotia's best-known culinary creation, the donair, is a local take a gyro or shawarma. Halifax's version distinguishes itself with a sweet sauce made up of evaporated milk, sugar and garlic. While these pita wrapped sandwiches are available all over the province, King of Donair on Pizza Corner in Halifax claims to be original home of the popular snack.

There are plenty of Chinese food restaurants located throughout the

Did you know...

that Joel Plaskett Emergency's album "Ashtray Rock" was named after a local landmark in the woods of Clayton Park where teenagers would go to drink and hang out?

province. The Hamachi House restaurants offer some of the best Japanese food in the province, while Thai and Indian cuisine is also available. In recent years Halifax has become a focal point for upscale dining in the province. Most of the better-known restaurants like the Press Gang, Chives and Seven are located downtown. The Hydro Stone market in the North End is also home to several top-notch eateries.

Bio ELLEN PAGE

Ellen Philpotts-Page was born on February 21, 1987, the daughter of a teacher and a graphic designer. With one roll, Page went from just another member of young Hollywood to the "It Girl."

Page got her start acting while still attending the Halifax Grammar School in the made-for-TV movie *Pit Pony*. At 16, she began working on small independent films, and then landing a role as Kitty Pryde in the third big budget X-Men movie. She gained critical acclaim in the movie *Hard Candy* about a sexual predator and the 14-year-old girl he tries to ensnare.

She followed this dark psychological thriller with a lighter role as the pregnant title character in Jason Reitman's *Juno*. Page won near-unanimous critical acclaim for her portrayal of the precocious teenager and landed an appearance on *The Late Show with David Letterman* and hosting duties on *Saturday Night Live*. She also scored an Academy Award nomination, a Golden Globe nomination, and a Screen Actor's Guild Award nomination. Even Roger Ebert, one of the biggest movie critics of all time, claimed, "Has there been a better performance this year than Ellen Page's creation of *Juno*? I don't think so."

Throughout the media frenzy, Page has bucked the pitfalls that befall many in young Hollywood and has remained an ambassador for the province, name-dropping businesses and landmarks in many interviews.

FAST FOOD

- Number of Tim Horton's in Canada: 2,733
- Number of Tim Horton's in Nova Scotia: 175
- Number of McDonald's in Canada: 1,400
- Number of McDonald's in Nova Scotia: 49
- Number of Subway's in Canada: 2,311
- Number of Subway's in Nova Scotia: 73

SPORTS

Although Nova Scotia doesn't have any major professional sports teams, athletics are still incredibly popular in the province. Like most of Canada, hockey is probably the most popular sport in the province. Both the Cape Breton Screaming Eagles and the Halifax Mooseheads are members of the Quebec Major Junior Hockey League, from which

They Said It

"In Dublin, we sold 54,000 tickets for a concert with Celine in a stadium in June. So, if we are not welcome in Halifax, we won't go there."
— Celine Dion's husband and manager Rene Angelil on why Celine cancelled her planned show on the Halifax Commons after some residents expressed their displeasure with Celine and her music.

the National Hockey League drafts many of its players.

There are also numerous teams in lower or recreational leagues. Basketball also has a strong following in the province. The Halifax Windjammers were successful in the early 1990s but unfortunately the World Basketball and the National Basketball Leagues they played in weren't and they went belly-up. The Halifax Rainmen made their debut in the American Basketball Association in the fall of 2007.

There is also a strong following for the various sports teams asso-

Take 5 CRAIG NORTON'S TOP FIVE FAVOURITE RESTAURANTS

Craig Norton is Director of Operations for the Prince George Hotel and restaurant GIO, as well as a Certified Sommelier with the International Sommelier Guild. He is a graduate of the Culinary Institute of Canada and a hard-core "foodie" with 20 years of experience in the hospitality industry.

1. **FID (Dresden Row, Halifax):** Here is a chef [Dennis Johnston] dedicated to the use of seasonal local ingredients, prepared simply to let the flavours speak. No one cooks salmon like Dennis.

2. **The Quarterdeck (Summerville Beach, South Shore):** The chowder and warm cheddar/jalapeno pepper tea biscuits – the chowder is full of seafood and add in the relaxed maritime friendly service with a view.

3. **Charlotte Lane (Shelburne):** Quaint Maritime hospitality with excellent food.

4. **Restaurant Le Caveau (Domaine de Grande Pre):** In the summer time, outside, under the pergola having Pork Schnitzel and L'Acadie Blanc Reserve… nothing better!

5. **Trattoria della Nonna (Lunenburg):** Italian food on the South Shore - just wicked!

ciated with Nova Scotia's many universities, with Saint Mary's Huskies Football being the most popular. Besides the more competitive spectator sports, recreational leagues for everything from Ultimate Frisbee to competitive dancing exist in the province.

Bio SIDNEY CROSBY

After playing just three seasons, Cole Harbour's Sidney Crosby has become the National Hockey League's most recognizable player. Crosby began playing hockey in his parent's basement at the age of two and was skating by three.

Throughout his teenage years Crosby won many MVP and scoring titles and in 2003 led his high school team to the US championships. In 2003, he was drafted by the Rimouski Oceanic to the QMJHL. After meeting Crosby and seeing him play, Wayne Gretzky said Crosby was the best hockey player he'd seen since Mario Lemieux. That praise would be prophetic in July of 2005 when the Pittsburgh Penguins, who Lemieux both owned and played for, drafted Crosby first overall in the NHL entry draft.

Before playing a single game in the NHL he signed several lucrative endorsement contracts including one with Reebok. Crosby's playing lived up to the hype – he netted 102 points in his rookie season, but lost the Calder Trophy, awarded to the league's "Rookie of the Year" to the Washington Capital's Alexander Ovechkin.

He finished the 2006-07 season with 120 points, winning the league's MVP and points awards, becoming the youngest player to do so. Despite his glowing success, Crosby continues to return to Nova Scotia in the off seasons, living in his hometown of Cole Harbour.

Take 5 TOP FIVE SPORTS ARENAS
BY SEATING CAPACITY

1. **Saint Mary's University Huskies Stadium** (12,000 seats)
2. **Halifax Metro Centre** (10,000 seats)
3. **Halifax Forum** (5,900 seats)
4. **Dartmouth Sportsplex** (5,100 seats)
5. **Centre 200** (5,000 seats)

COMMUNICATIONS
TV stations: 4
Radio stations: 68
Daily newspapers: 6

Weblinks

Nova Scotia Department of Tourism, Culture and Heritage – Culture Division
www.gov.ns.ca/dtc/culture/default.asp
Government website for all things culture related in the province, including information on grants and funding for the arts.

Halifax Locals
www.halifaxlocals.com
A clearing house for the goings-on in Halifax's diverse music scene. The sight is heavily slanted towards the local scene and is the best place to find out who's playing where and when.

The Coast
www.thecoast.ca
The Internet home of Halifax's alternative-weekly newspaper. *The Coast* covers everything from local news to food, music and movies. It's the best source for upcoming events in and around Metro Halifax.

Economy

Nova Scotia's economy has traditionally been a resource-based one, with the fishing industry being the best known outside of the province. However, since the collapse of the fishing industry in 1992, the economy has diversified to include manufacturing and tourism as major breadwinners. Of course, mining of gypsum, salt and barite, logging and farming are still major components of Nova Scotia's GDP. After years of exploration, offshore drilling for oil and gas is starting to pay off and the province will see an increase in natural gas revenues as exploration continues.

GDP (2006)

Gross Domestic Product represents the total value of goods and services produced.

- Total GDP: $31,997,000
- GDP per capita: $34,210
- Canadian GDP per capita: $44,109
- Nova Scotia GDP growth: 0.9 percent
- Canadian GDP growth: 2.8 percent

Source: Stats Can

TAXES

- Provincial sales tax: 8 percent
- GST (federal sales tax): 5 percent
- Personal income tax rate: 8.79 percent on the first $29,590 of taxable income; 14.95 percent on the next $29,590; 16.67 percent on the next $33,820; 17.5 percent on the amount over $93,000
- Small business tax rate: 5 percent
- Corporate tax rate: 16 percent

Source: Canada Customs and Revenue Agency

TAX FREEDOM DAY

Tax freedom day (date on which earnings no longer go to taxes, 2008) is June 19 nationally.

- Alberta: June 1
- New Brunswick: June 14
- Prince Edward Island: June 14
- Saskatchewan: June 14
- Manitoba: June 16
- British Columbia: June 16
- Nova Scotia: June 19
- Ontario: June 19
- Newfoundland and Labrador: July 1
- Quebec: July 26

Did you know...

that when Nova Scotia joined Confederation in 1867, it was the wealthiest province in Canada?

You Said How Much?

Select hourly wages in Nova Scotia, taken from the latest available data.

Judge:	$90.44
University Professor:	$36.24
Pharmacist:	$34.50
High School Teacher:	$31.62
Police Officer:	$30.77
Accountant:	$30.20
Elementary School Teacher:	$28.72
Veterinarian:	$28.60
Registered Nurse:	$27.53
Librarian:	$25.46
Social Worker:	$24.84
Journalist:	$21.73
Plumber:	$21.50
Psychologist:	$19.80
Carpenter:	$18.50
Firefighter:	$18.46
Executive Assistant:	$16.50
Chef:	$16.30
Religious Minister:	$16.25
Truck Driver:	$16.00
Photographer:	$15.89
Event Planner:	$14.07
Secretary:	$13.75
Retail Sales Associate:	$9.35
Cook:	$9.00
Bartender:	$8.13
Server:	$7.85

1. Clerical
2. Sales and Service
3. Management (non-senior)
4. Retail sales, clerks, cashiers
5. Machine operators and assemblers

HOUSEHOLD INCOME

The median household income in Canada after taxes was $45,900 in 2005.

- Calgary: $56,600
- Toronto: $55,400
- Winnipeg: $44,900
- Halifax: $42,900
- Vancouver: $49,200
- Quebec City: $42,000
- Montreal: $40,700

Source: Canada Mortgage and Housing Corporation

BY THE HOUR

In 2007, workers in Nova Scotia earned an average hourly salary of $18.10, up 6.9 percent from 2006.

- Aged 15 to 24: $10.67
- Aged 25 to 54: $19.47
- Aged 55 and older: $20.51
- Men: $19.82
- Women: $16.48
- Part-time: $13.10
- Full-time: $19.26
- Unionized: $22.38
- Non-unionized: $16.28

WHERE THE MONEY GOES

Nova Scotian households spend an average of $56,105 a year. Here's how it breaks down:

* Income tax: $10,207 (18 percent)

Bio ROY JODREY

Roy A. Jodrey belongs to the familiar group of early Nova Scotia entrepreneurs who raised themselves up by their bootstraps, compensating for their lack of education with sheer determination and street smarts.

Before Jodrey left school at the age of 12 in Hantsport, Annapolis County, legend has it that he'd already started two business ventures (he built himself his own water mill to make and sell apple cider and sold blueberries door-to-door). When he left school, it didn't mean the end of learning; he devoured books on farming, finance, and hydropower, all of which would play a crucial role in business ventures in the future.

By 16, Jodrey was working in his father's apple orchard; by 18, he'd transformed his father's business, shipping apples to new markets in New England. Still in his twenties, Jodrey built a water dam that would produce power for the Annapolis Valley. When he felt power consumption had lagged expectation, he sold electrical appliances.

Other dams and a power company would be followed by businesses as diverse as paper, food processing, manufacturing, flower, transportation, real estate development, environmental and waste treatment, metal finishing, specialized coatings and health care. In 1945, Jodrey formed Scotia Investments Limited, an investment holding company to manage the company's interests. He passed away at the age of 84 in 1973.

The Jodrey family is by far the richest of all Nova Scotia families. Estimates of the wealth vary but it is believed to be around $340 million, versus, say, the Sobey family, which is estimated to be worth in the neighbourhood of $180 million.

- Shelter: $10,097 (18 percent)
- Transportation: $7,922 (14 percent)
- Food: $6,403 (11 percent)
- Insurance/pension payments: $3,388 (6 percent)
- Household operation: $3,081 (5 percent)
- Clothing: $2,087 (4 percent)
- Monetary gifts/contributions: $1,471 (2.5 percent)
- Health care: $1,693 (3 percent)
- Tobacco and alcohol: $1,468 (2.5 percent)
- Education: $1,012 (2 percent)
- Personal care: $965 (2 percent)
- Reading material: $263 (0.5 percent)
- Games of chance: $320 (0.5 percent)

Source: Stats Can

They Said It

"I was associated with Roy Jodrey for 43 years. I know of no man who taught me so much; I know of no man who contributed so much to Nova Scotia, and I know of no man who had higher principles in his dealings with people. He was a man whose word was as good as his bond."

– Frank Covert, one of Canada's most skilled corporate lawyers

Take 5 TOP FIVE INTERNATIONAL EXPORTS

1. **Non-metallic minerals, mineral fuels**
2. **Fish and fish products**
3. **Tires**
4. **Paper and paperboard**
5. **Agriculture products and food**

Source: NS Department of Agriculture

BUYING A HOUSE

Canada (average cost): $162,709
Newfoundland and Labrador: $76,283
New Brunswick: $86,538
Saskatchewan: $93,065
Manitoba: $97,670
Prince Edward Island: $100,657
Nova Scotia: $101,515
Quebec: $110,668
Alberta: $159,698
Ontario: $199,884
British Columbia: $230,645

Source: Statistics Canada, Canadian Real Estate Association

RENTING

- Average monthly rent paid in the province: $731
- Average vacancy rate in 2007: 3.2 percent

Did you know...

that Canada's first coal mine opened in Cape Breton in 1720?

Take 5 — TOP FIVE SHELLFISH/ CRUSTACEAN EXPORTS

1. **Lobster:** $390 million
2. **Shrimp:** $106 million
3. **Scallops:** $92 million
4. **Crab:** $81.4 million
5. **Clams:** $8.6 million

Source: NS Department of Agriculture

RENTS IN SELECTED METRO AREAS

City	1 bedroom	2 bedrooms
Halifax	**$659**	**$815**
Montreal	$562	$616
Edmonton	$608	$732
Calgary	$666	$808
Ottawa	$762	$920
Vancouver	$788	$1,004
Toronto	$888	$1,052

Source: Canada Mortgage and Housing Corporation.

WHERE WE WORK

- The median distance of Nova Scotians from their work place is 7.8 km.
- 75 percent drive their own vehicles to work, 9.6 percent carpool, 8 percent walk, 5 percent take public transit.
- Percentage of Nova Scotians who work at home: 6.7 percent
- Percentage who work a standard 35-40 hour week: 57
- Percentage who work more than 50 hours a week: 16.4

Did you know...

that the largest recorded lobster was caught off southern Nova Scotia in 1977? It weighed in at 44 lb. 6 oz. and measured 3 ft. 6 in. from the end of the tail to the tip of the largest claw.

Take 5 TOP FIVE FINFISH EXPORTS

1. **Cod:** $40 million
2. **Haddock:** $29 million
3. **Hake:** $28 million
4. **Halibut:** $23 million
5. **Mackerel:** $15 million

Source: NS Department of Agriculture

UNEMPLOYMENT (2007)

- Unemployment rate in Nova Scotia: 7.1 percent
- Unemployment rate in Halifax Metro, the lowest in the province: 3.9 percent
- Unemployment rate in Cape Breton, the highest: 12.8 percent

SMALL BUSINESS

In 2004, thirty percent of the Nova Scotia workforce worked for a small business with fewer than 50 employees, according to the Canadian Federation of Independent Business.

- Percentage of small businesses that start from scratch: 58
- Percentage that start with the purchase of an existing business: 22
- Percentage that start as the result of taking over a family business: 15
- Percentage that are spin-offs of other businesses: 4
- Percentage located in towns and villages: 38
- Percentage in rural Nova Scotia: 26
- Percentage located in downtown urban areas: 20
- Percentage located in the suburbs: 16

Source: Canadian Federation of Small Business

Bluefin

The magnificent Atlantic bluefin tuna was not always held in the esteem it is today. Until the 1930s, it was considered a nuisance fish, preying on the much more valuable cod and herring stocks. In Nova Scotia, if they were caught at all, it was to eliminate their effect on the other fisheries. They literally sold for pennies to cat food manufactures, or were ploughed into the soil for fertilizer.

Today, even non-fishers' eyes alight at the word bluefin. And why wouldn't they? Even if it didn't make it to the world's trendy sushi restaurants, its sheer size and speed would guarantee it public interest. It is the world's largest bony fish, reaching over half a ton in weight, and today fetching more than $150,000 a fish. It has been known to dive to depths of up to 500 m and is an inveterate traveller. Tagged bluefin have been tracked swimming 7,500 km across the Atlantic in 119 days, meaning if they were swimming in a straight line they would be putting in 65 km a day.

It was the Americans who first flocked to the small Nova Scotia fishing village of Wedgeport to pursue the ultimate trophy fish that ultimately alerted the local population to its potential value. People like Ernest Hemingway, business magnate Michael Lerner, Amelia Earhart, Kate Smith and Franklin D. Roosevelt all came in pursuit of the big game fish.

Atlantic bluefin landed in Nova Scotia are still famous, only now they are eaten by humans instead of cats. From June through October, the period when they are off the Nova Scotia coast, they can increase their body mass by 40 percent. A Nova Scotian, Ken Fraser, holds the world record for the largest bluefin catch, a 1,496-pounder he hooked on October 26th, 1979 off Auld's Cove.

Did you know...

MANUFACTURING

Approximately ten percent of the Nova Scotia economy is accounted for by manufacturing. The value of the goods manufactured and exported annually is fast approaching $9 billion.

- Percentage of employed Nova Scotians who work in manufacturing: 11
- Top three manufacturing industries in the province: food industries, refined petroleum/coal industries and transportation equipment industries

TIRES

On October 3, 2000, Michelin North America's three Nova Scotian plants at Bridgewater, Granton and Waterville produced its 150 millionth tire. They have since expanded both the Waterville and Bridgewater production facilities, creating over 100 new jobs.

- Number of years it took the company to produce their first 50 million tires: 15
- The second 50 million tires: 8 years
- The third 50 million tires: 5 years
- Number of Nova Scotians who work for Michelin: 3,500
- Rank as the largest Nova Scotian employer: 4th

Did you know...

that with an injury frequency rate of 5 percent, fishing was the most dangerous industry in Nova Scotia for on-the-job injuries in 2006?

MINING

Nova Scotia's mining industry is worth just over $286 million to the Nova Scotia economy - our mining history includes the production of gypsum, anhydrite, salt, aggregate, barite, coal, gold, copper, lead, zinc, tin, antimony, manganese, and several others. Highlights of current production include:

- 8 million tonnes of gypsum annually from 5 mines (80% of total Canadian production)
- 1 million tonnes of salt annually from 1 underground mine and 1 brining operation (10% of total Canadian production)
- 10 million tonnes of crushed stone, sand and gravel per year
- 0.3-0.4 million tonnes of coal per year from five mines

Source: Nova Scotia Natural Resources

OFFSHORE OIL AND GAS

The offshore oil industry contributes more than $1 billion to the Nova Scotia GDP every year.

- Year in which Mobil Oil Canada received the first offshore license to explore for gas off Nova Scotia, in the Sable Island block: 1959
- Number of wells that had been drilled off Nova Scotia by 2001: 140
- Number of these that resulted in significant discoveries: 22
- Year gas started flowing from the Sable Offshore Energy Project Five: 1999
- Average number of cubic feet of natural gas produced every day: 400 million
- Number of barrels of natural gas liquids produced every day: 20,000

Did you know...

that Nova Scotia is home to an estimated 3 billion tonnes of coal?

Bio ALEXANDER KEITH

Popular lore portrays Alexander Keith as the affable Haligonian who brought Nova Scotians their favorite beer. Television commercials take it a bit further, portraying him as a man who loved a good folk song and had a penchant for pretty bar wenches. The question is, who was the real Alexander Keith?

He was born in Scotland in October 1795, and as a teenager his father sent him to England to learn the brewing trade. At the age of 22, he immigrated to Halifax, where he worked for brewmaster Charles Boggs. By 1820, Keith bought out Boggs and began his career as a brewer. In 1822, he moved his business to Water Street, building Keith Hall in 1863.

Alexander Keith was very involved in the life of his booming young city, serving on various boards and associations. He was especially involved in the Freemasons, becoming a provincial Grand Master. In 1841, he was elected to city council, serving as mayor in 1853 and 1854. In 1843 he was appointed to the Nova Scotia Legislative Council, and at Confederation in 1867, pro-confederate Keith was offered, but declined, an appointment to the Canadian Senate.

Alexander Keith's life was not without controversy. During the American Civil War, many Haligonians, Keith among them, favored the cause of Southerners. Reportedly Keith helped Southern raiders escape capture off the northeast coast. Though unproven, it has been suggested that Keith was in fact a spy for the South. When Keith died in Halifax in December 1873, his estate was valued at $251,000.

Take 5 — TOP FIVE CONTAINER IMPORTS
TO THE PORT OF HALIFAX

1. **Machinery** – machinery, mechanical appliances, parts
2. **Building** – other ceramic products
3. **Chemicals** – other inorganic
4. **Miscellaneous manufactured goods**
5. **Furniture/lights/mattresses**

PORT OF HALIFAX

Halifax's deep, ice-free harbour makes it one of the most valuable in the country and a boon to the province's economy. Each year the port generates almost $700 million, and more than 9,000 Nova Scotians work directly and indirectly for it. In 2006, the port handled the equivalent of 530,772 twenty-foot cargo containers.

LOBSTER

Lobster caught in Atlantic waters is highly favoured as the cadillac of lobster and is Nova Scotia's most valuable species.

- Total weight of lobster caught in 2006: 22,471 tonnes
- Total value of the catch: $390.3 million

Source: NS Lobster Council

Did you know...

that Nova Scotia maple trees yield more than 140,000 liters of maple syrup each year?

Did you know...

that Nova Scotia is the world's largest exporter of lobsters, Christmas trees, gypsum, carrots, and strawberry plants?

Take 5 — TOP FIVE CONTAINER EXPORTS
FROM THE PORT OF HALIFAX

1. Newsprint
2. Machinery/mechanical appliances/parts
3. Wood/wood pulp
4. Vegetables
5. Paper

A FISH STORY

The fishery continues to be a profitable industry for the province and is Canada's second leading exporter of fish and seafood products, having a value of over $974 million.

AGRICULTURE

The combined farm gate value of Nova Scotian-grown agricultural products is more than $450 million annually. More than 10,000 Nova Scotians are directly employed by agriculture and around ten percent of Nova Scotia's workforce is somehow connected to the agri-food industry.

Source: NS Department of Agriculture

DAIRY

Of the 3,923 farms in Nova Scotia, 1,705 have dairy cows. There are approximately 107,000 cows in the province, 22,900 of which are dairy cows. Milk and cream sales alone fetch more than $100 million annually.

Did you know...

that Sobeys is the only Nova Scotia business that numbers in the top 50 largest employers in Canada?

TOP FIVE FARMING COUNTIES
IN NOVA SCOTIA (NUMBER OF FARMS)

1. **Kings County:** 644
2. **Cumberland:** 539
3. **Colchester:** 452
4. **Lunenburg:** 370
5. **Hants:** 336

WILD BLUEBERRIES

Nova Scotia is the world's second largest exporter of wild blueberries behind Maine, USA. This crop is sold in markets in the U.S., Germany, Japan, France, United Kingdom, Scandinavia, Italy, Netherlands, Switzerland, Taiwan, Caribbean, and Australia. In 2006, 35,300 hectares of wild blueberries were grown in Nova Scotia, worth more than $23,235,000 to farmers.

EGGS

Nova Scotia farms have more than 738,000 laying chickens. They produce more than 18 million dozen eggs, hatching a tidy $22.5 million annually.

They Said It

"I learned more about sound business practices from Pictou County farmers than I could have learned from any other place."
— B. Frank Sobey

Take 5 TOP FIVE TOURISM-DOLLAR GENERATING REGIONS IN NOVA SCOTIA

1. **Halifax-Dartmouth:** $623 million
2. **Cape Breton:** $212.5 million
3. **Annapolis Valley:** $167 million
4. **South Shore:** $112 million
5. **Northumberland Shore:** $99 million

Source: NS Department of Tourism

FORESTRY AND LOGGING

- Millions of cords of wood harvested annually in Nova Scotia: 2
- Exports of forest products annually: Over $1.1 billion
- Rank of Nova Scotia as a Canadian producer of pulp and paper: 5
- Number of Nova Scotians working in jobs directly related to the forestry industry: 11,900

OH CHRISTMAS TREE

More than 2,500 people grow Christmas trees in Nova Scotia, farming 10,000 hectares of land. Each year, nearly two million trees are sent to market, generating $30 million. 80 percent of the trees are exported to the US. The Balsam Fir reigns as king of Nova Scotia's Christmas tree industry, covering 99 percent of the total market.

Did you know...

that Nova Scotia was home to Canada's first decorated Christmas tree in 1846?

WINE, SPIRIT, AND BEER PRODUCERS

Nova Scotia has a number of winemaking operations, as well as breweries and distilleries. A number of these vineyards, wineries, breweries, and distilleries offer tours of their vineyards and/or production facilities and sell their products directly to the public on site.

- Bear River Vineyards, Bear River
- Rudder's Brew Pub, Yarmouth
- Blomidon Estate Winery, Canning
- Lunenburg County Winery, Newburne
- Gaspereau Vineyards, Gaspereau
- Domain de Grande Pre, Grande Pre
- Sainte-Famille Wines, Falmouth
- Keltic Brewing Company Ltd, Truro
- Jost Vineyards, Malagash
- Williamsdale Winery, Williamsdale
- Olands Brewery, Halifax
- Sleeman's Maritimes, Dartmouth
- Keith's Brewery, Halifax
- Garrison Brewery, Halifax
- Propeller Brewery, Halifax
- The Granite Brewery, Halifax
- Rogue's Roast, Halifax
- Chedabucto Bay Brewery, Guysborough
- Glenora Distillery, Glenville

Source: NSLC

Did you know...

that Nova Scotia is one of the world's top fur producers? There are 109 mink farms and 10 fox farms alone. The 762,100 mink pelts and 1,100 fox pelts produced in the province last year were worth $54 million.

SELLING CANADA'S OCEAN PLAYGROUND

In 2007, tourism injected $ 1.3 billion into the provincial economy.

- Number of people who visited Nova Scotia in 2006: 2.12 million
- Percentage who came from elsewhere in Canada: 30
- Number of Atlantic Canadians who visited the province, accounting for 55 percent of all visitors: 1.16 million
- Percentage from the United States: 11.4
- Percentage from overseas: 3.6

Source: NS Department of Tourism

Weblinks

HRDC Job Bank

http://www.jobbank.gc.ca/Search_en.

Follow the links to find hundreds of job openings in your area from this website, which is updated daily.

Nova Scotia Online: Real Estate

www.nsonline.com/business/real_estate/

Find real estate listings from several realtors from all over the province.

Nova Scotia Organic Growers Association

www.nsoga.org

This organization certifies organic farms and businesses in the province; their website includes information about the certification process and standards, an updated growers list, the board of directors, and more.

Did you know...

that in Nova Scotia, dairy cows produce 1,923,171 eight-ounce glasses of milk a day?

Politics

With the Treaty of Paris in 1763, France essentially ceded political domain to England for all of North America. Initially, Cape Breton Island, Prince Edward Island, and New Brunswick were joined to Nova Scotia, but in 1769, Prince Edward Island was separated from Nova Scotia, as were Cape Breton Island and New Brunswick in 1784. Cape Breton Island would be re-annexed in 1820.

Nova Scotia achieved present day Canada's first representative assembly, with elections taking place for the first time in 1758 in Halifax. Nova Scotia was far from democratic, but it at least now had a bicameral legislature that included an elected house of assembly. Although the elected assembly clamoured for more and more authority, it was the council appointed by the Crown that had final legislative, judicial, and executive powers.

REFORMERS

By 1820, reformers were demanding responsible government, meaning they wanted real autonomy for the legislative branch. The leader who would make it happen was the influential orator and publisher, Joseph Howe, who used his newspaper and his powerful speaking skills to challenge the governor. In 1848, the governor finally relented and Nova Scotia became the first British colony to obtain responsible government.

CANADA CALLING

Great Britain was looking for a way to maintain some influence in North America and at the same time create a counterpoint to the increasingly powerful American democracy. The solution was to consolidate their North American sphere of influence in the British North America Act, in effect creating the country of Canada.

Support for Confederation in Nova Scotia was tepid. Nova Scotia's elite saw their fortunes more closely entwined with that of Great Britain than with a newly imagined country. When the first election was called, 18 of the 19 Nova Scotians elected to the new federal House of Commons opposed Confederation.

The chief opposition spokesman was none other than Joseph Howe. In the end, however, the forces aligned against Howe and his colleagues were just too huge to overcome.

BUT HE SAID . . .

"He appeared deeply impressed by my statements, and said great many civil things, but expressed his fears that if he took that course his party would abandon him."

—Charles Tupper, in an April 9, 1868 letter to John A. Macdonald, describing an earlier meeting with Joseph Howe in which he had tried to convince Howe to abandon his anti-Confederation stance.

They Said It

"The few members who watched the British North America Act in its speedy passage through parliament could scarcely conceal their excruciating boredom, and after the ordeal was over, they turned with lively zeal and manifest relief to the great national problem of the tax on dogs."

– Historian Donald Creighton's take on the 'momentous' signing of the BNA Act, in *The Victorians and the Empire*, 1937

Take 5 DR. J. MURRAY BECK'S
FIVE MOST IMPORTANT POLITICAL FIGURES IN NOVA SCOTIA HISTORY

Born in Lunenburg in 1914, Dr. J. Murray Beck has taught and written extensively on Canadian and Nova Scotian government and political history. He is Professor Emeritus of Political Science at Dalhousie University. Among his books are *Joseph Howe, Vol. I* and *Vol. II, the Government of Nova Scotia*, and the two-volume *Politics of Nova Scotia*.

1. **Joseph Howe:** Led a non-violent reform movement in Nova Scotia during the 1830s and 1840s. As a result, in February 1848, the province became the first colony in the British Empire to achieve responsible government.

2. **Robert L. Stanfield:** As Premier of Nova Scotia from 1956 to 1967, Robert Stanfield's successful promotion of industrial development led to his recognition as a prime mover in building the 'new Nova Scotia.' As opposition leader at Ottawa between 1967 and 1976, he won the reputation of being "the best prime minister Canada never had."

3. **Angus L. Macdonald:** Premier of Nova Scotia from 1933 to 1940 and from 1945 to 1954, had a natural eloquence and gifts of intellect and judgment leading to "a wide personal following not seen in the province since the days of Howe." Perhaps his hold over Nova Scotians was even stronger than that of Howe.

4. **George H. Murray:** Even in the absence of polls, he had an uncanny aptitude for gauging the attitudes and sensibilities of the Nova Scotia people. That enabled him to win six successive elections and hold the premiership for twenty-six years from 1896 to 1923, a time still unequalled in the annals of British parliamentary government.

5. **Sir Robert Borden:** Headed the government of Canada during the First World War. Under him, the country took tentative steps leading in the next decade to full Canadian autonomy.

"He thinks the Canadians will offer us any terms, and that he and I combined might rule the Dominion. Of course I gave him no satisfaction."
—Joseph Howe's decidedly less enthusiastic interpretation of this same meeting with Tupper, in a letter to Macdonald dated April 9, 1868.

POST CONFEDERATION

In 1928, Nova Scotia abolished its appointed council, in effect vesting all legislative authority in the elected assembly. The province operates in the British parliamentary tradition with the government staying in power as long as it has the support of the majority of the members of the legislature. There are no fixed dates for elections, but tradition dictates that a government cannot go without calling an election within five years of the beginning of its mandate.

PARTIES

Two main political parties in Nova Scotia, the Liberal Party and the Progressive Conservative Party, have governed the province since its entry into Canada. The Liberals have been in power the lion's share of the time. During the 20th century, the Liberals governed until 1925, from 1933 to 1956, 1970 to 1978, and 1993 to 1999; the Progressive Conservatives were in power during the other periods.

The Progressive Conservatives regained control of the provincial government in 1999. In the late 1990s, the New Democratic Party (NDP) increased its share of seats in the House of Assembly. The Conservatives remained in power after the 2006 provincial election, though they are a minority government. Under the leadership of Rodney MacDonald, the party won 22 seats in the 52-seat provincial legislature.

Did you know...

that Premier Rodney MacDonald previously worked as a teacher and a professional musician, receiving two nominations for East Coast Music Awards?

Take 5 PREMIER RODNEY MACDONALD'S
FIVE FAVOURITE NOVA SCOTIANS

Rodney MacDonald was born January 2, 1972 in Inverness, Nova Scotia. Upon graduating from high school in Mabou, Inverness County, MacDonald earned a Bachelor of Science in Physical Education from St. Francis Xavier University.

MacDonald was elected to Nova Scotia Legislature July 1999 as the MLA for Inverness. In February 2006, MacDonald won the leadership race for the Nova Scotia Progressive Conservative party and was sworn in as the province's 33rd premier. Nova Scotians re-elected MacDonald as premier in 2006.

1. **John Hamm:** His courage and conviction to balance the budget for the first time in 40 years has given our province a better, more prosperous future.

2. **Alex Angus MacDonald:** My father influenced me greatly over the course of my life. A municipal councillor and pipefitter, his advice and example provided me with direction both personally and professionally.

3. **Maud Lewis:** Her physical challenges due to arthritis and polio did not discourage her efforts to express her artistic talents. Her paintings indicate a positive spirit revealing the simple everyday beauty of life.

4. **Angus L. MacDonald:** Young, impressive, well educated and highly charismatic, his leadership brought stability to Nova Scotia through the Depression era. One of his greatest achievements was the establishment of a public education system for all Nova Scotians.

5. **Al MacInnis:** Al has had a spectacular career and will be regarded as one of the NHL's finest defensemen of all time. He had talent, but he also dedicated himself to the discipline of hard work. He went on to win the Stanley Cup and Conn Smythe Trophy as playoff MVP, as well as the Norris Trophy as the NHL's best defenseman.

Bio ANGUS L. MACDONALD

Born to a farming family in Dunvegan, Cape Breton in August 1890, Angus Lewis Macdonald was the ninth of fourteen children. Always studious, as a teenager Macdonald worked a range of jobs, saving every penny to pay his tuition at St. Francis Xavier University.

With the outbreak of World War I, Macdonald quickly enlisted. Just four days before Armistice, he was shot and critically wounded. When he regained his health, he returned to Nova Scotia, enrolling at Dalhousie Law School. He excelled at law school and, not long after graduating, became a popular law professor.

In 1930, Macdonald reluctantly accepted the leadership of the Nova Scotia Liberals. By 1933, he and his party handily won the provincial election with a mandate promising an Old Age Pension Act, support for workers' rights to unionize, and a plan to reduce government expenditures.

During the Second World War, Macdonald handed off his premiership to Alexander MacMillan while he served in Ottawa as federal Minister of National Defence and Naval Services. In 1945, Macdonald returned to Nova Scotia politics, and, with the campaign slogan "All's well with Angus L" was again elected premier, this time with the largest mandate in Nova Scotia history.

Macdonald responded to calls for improved education for Nova Scotians by creating the province's first Department of Education. He embarked on major construction projects, including the first bridge connecting Halifax and Dartmouth, and the Canso Causeway. In the 1953 election, Macdonald was again elected. On April 11, 1954, 63-year old Macdonald had a heart attack, dying in his sleep two days later. Shocked Nova Scotians publicly mourned his death. In a state funeral held in Halifax, tens of thousands came to pay their final respects.

The NDP sits in the official opposition with 20 seats and the Liberals have nine seats. There is currently one independent MLA in the Nova Scotia Legislature. The Nova Scotia Green Party received official party status in April of 2006. It ran a full slate of candidates in the provincial election that year and, though it didn't win any seats in the legislature, it did received 2.3 percent of the popular vote. The current Green Party leader is Ken McGowan.

Source: Nova Scotia Legislature

CURRENT ADMINISTRATION
- Premier: Rodney MacDonald, the 33rd
- Party: Progressive Conservatives
- Number of seats won: 22
- Number of Liberal seats won: 9 (Stephen McNeil)
- Number of NDP seats won: 20 (Darrel Dexter)
- Date of latest election: June 13, 2006
- Voter turnout: 61.65% (405,716 people voted of a possible 658,055 eligible voters)

Did you know...

that George H. Murray was the longest serving premier in Nova Scotian and Canadian history, serving for 27 consecutive years from 1896 until finally resigning in 1923?

Did you know...

that Premier John Thompson was the first Catholic Conservative Premier of Nova Scotia and the first Catholic Prime Minister of Canada? His religion prevented him from directly succeeding Sir John A. MacDonald.

PREMIERS

NAME	PARTY	PROFESSION	SERVED
James Uniacke	Reformer	Politician	1848-1854
William Young	Liberal	Lawyer	1854-1857
James Johnston	Conservative	Lawyer	1857-1860
William Young	Liberal	Lawyer	Feb-Aug 1860
Joseph Howe	Liberal	Newspaper Editor	1860-1863
James Johnston	Conservative	Lawyer	1863-1864
Charles Tupper	Conservative	Medical Doctor	1864-1867
Hiram Blanchard	(Confederate) Conservative	Lawyer	July-Sept 1867
William Annand	(Anti-confederate) Liberal	Farmer, Newspaper Editor	1867-75
Philip Hill	Liberal	Lawyer, Former Mayor of Halifax	1875-78
Simon Holmes	Conservative	Lawyer, Newspaper Editor	1878-82
Sir John Thompson	Conservative	Lawyer	May-July 1882
William Pipes	Liberal	Lawyer	1882-84
William Fielding	Liberal	Newspaper Editor	1884-96
George H. Murray	Liberal	Lawyer	1896-1923

PREMIERS CONTINUED

NAME	PARTY	PROFESSION	SERVED
Ernest Armstrong	Liberal	Lawyer	1923-25
Edgar Rhodes	Conservative	Lawyer	1925-30
Gordon Harrington	Conservative	Lawyer	1930-35
Angus L. MacDonald	Liberal	Barrister, Lecturer, Professor	1933-40;1945-54
Alexander MacMillan	Liberal	Businessman	1940-45
Harold Connolly	Liberal	Newspaper Editor	April-Sept 1954
Henry Hicks	Liberal	Lawyer	1954-56
Robert Stanfield	Conservative	Lawyer	1956-67
George I. Smith	Conservative	Lawyer	1967-70
Gerald Regan	Liberal	Lawyer	1970-78
John Buchanan	Conservative	Lawyer	1978-90
Roger Bacon	Conservative	Farmer	1990-91
Donald Cameron	Conservative	Farmer	1991-93
John Savage	Liberal	Medical Doctor	1993-97
Russell MacLellan	Liberal	Lawyer	1997-99
John Hamm	Conservative	Medical Doctor	1999-2006
Rodney MacDonald	Conservative	PE Teacher/Fiddler	2006-present

WOMEN IN POLITICS

- 1918: Women receive the right to vote in provincial elections. The right to run for political office is also granted.
- 1946: Gladys Porter is elected Mayor of Kentville, making her the first female mayor in all of Eastern Canada.
- 1960: Gladys Porter becomes Nova Scotia's first female MLA after she is elected in the Kings-North Riding as a Progressive Conservative. She serves until her death in 1967.
- 1981: Alexa McDonough becomes Nova Scotia's first female leader of a major political party when she wins leadership of the NDP.
- 2000: Myra Freeman is sworn in as Nova Scotia's first female Lieutenant Governor.
- There is currently 1 female senator and 1 female MP in Ottawa from Nova Scotia.

FEDERAL POLITICS

- Number of Nova Scotians who have been Prime Minister: 3 (John Thompson, Charles Tupper and Robert Borden)
- Current number of MPs in Ottawa: 11
- Current number of Senators: 7

Did you know...

that Prime Minister John Thompson died on his 50th birthday, November 10, 1894, from a sudden stroke during lunch at Windsor Castle, after being knighted that morning by Queen Victoria? His death challenged royal protocol. After holding a requiem mass for him at the castle, the Queen insisted his body be transported back to Canada with due pomp and ceremony. The HMS Blenheim was painted black for the journey across the Atlantic to Halifax, where a state funeral took place on January 3, 1895.

Weblinks

PC Party of Nova Scotia

www.pcparty.ns.ca

The official website of Rodney MacDonald and the Nova Scotia PC Party.

Nova Scotia Liberal Party

www.liberal.ns.ca

The official website of Stephen MacNeil and the Nova Scotia Liberal Party.

Nova Scotia NDP Party

www.ns.ndp.ca

The official website of Darrell Dexter and the NDP Party.

Green Party of Nova Scotia

www.greenparty.ns.ca

The official website of Ellen Durkee and the Green Party.

Did you know...

that former Premier Russell MacLellan has a Black Belt in TaeKwon Do?

Did you know...

that before Robert Stanfield was born, his family made a fortune selling the first unshrinkable underwear to Maritimers heading northwest to the Klondike Gold Rush? As a result, the young Robert never had to work, inheriting $350,000 at the age of 25 after his father died when he was 17.

Then and Now

From the pre-industrial age through to the modern age, one only need reflect back a generation to see just how much times have changed. From the early days of the Acadians to today's urban sprawl, this chapter is a walk back through time that shows where we came from.

POPULATION THEN AND NOW
(PERCENTAGE OF CANADIAN POPULATION)

1763: 13,000 (16.4%)
1850: 275 000 (11.4%)
1901: 460,000 (8.6%)
2006: 913,462 (2.8%)

Source: Stats Can

LIFE EXPECTANCY

Over the past century, the life expectancy of Nova Scotians has been on the rise. One thing that hasn't changed, however, is that our women outlive the men.

	Men	Women
1921	59.2	61.1
1971	68.7	76.0
2002	74.8	80.6

WAGES

Average weekly salary of Nova Scotians:
- 1939: $21.42
- 1959: $60.17
- 2005: $597.00

FARMING

Farming was once practiced by most Nova Scotians, either as a primary livelihood or part-time as a means of supplementing incomes and feeding families. Over the past century, the once-numerous Nova Scotia family farm has given way to fewer but larger, more efficient and mechanized farms.
- 1901 combined hectares of all Nova Scotia farms: 2,460,903
- In 1951: 1,284,477
- In 2001: 407,047

The output of efficient mammoth farms remains economically significant, but far fewer Nova Scotians live a farming lifestyle. In 1901, 52,836 Nova Scotians worked in agriculture. This number fell to 22,918 in 1951 and is approximately 9,000 today.

HOW 'BOUT THEM APPLES

Today, Nova Scotia apples are an important cash crop for the province. What many people don't know is that apples are not native to the province — they were introduced by Europeans in 1606. It was not until 1849 that Nova Scotia exported its first apples. Today, Nova Scotia produces 100 million pounds of apples and each May, Nova Scotians celebrate the fruit with the Apple Blossom Festival in the Annapolis Valley.

Did you know...

that Nova Scotia issued its first liquor license in 1749 to John Shippey's tavern, the Spread Eagle? The tavern still exists today, but is know known as the Split Crow.

EDUCATION

In 1780, the first Nova Scotia law mandated the creation of publicly funded schools for poor children; everyone else had to pay for their children's schooling. Universal free public education arrived in 1864. Up until the 1950s, most Nova Scotians were educated in one-room school

Halifax Explosion

December 6th, 1917 dawned a typical day in wartime Halifax as the harbour bustled with navy vessels, cargo ships and ferries. That morning, the Mont Blanc sailed into Halifax harbour, its cargo of explosives unmarked. As it approached its mooring, the Imo, a Belgian relief vessel, started down the harbour, crossing paths with the munitions ship.

Claiming the right-of-way, the Mont Blanc directed the Imo to move aside; the Imo stayed its course. In a final effort to avoid collision, the Mont Blanc veered left and the Imo threw its engines into reverse. It was too late and at 8:45 am the two ships collided, igniting a fire aboard the Mont Blanc. Unaware of the deadly cargo, land and sea crews worked to quell flames, but at 9:04 am, as Haligonians watched on, the Mont Blanc exploded.

The largest manmade blast in history rained red-hot iron and steel down on the city. Moments later, a tsunami swept ashore. Homes, schools and businesses within two square kilometers of the Halifax waterfront were immediately obliterated and others destroyed by gas-line fires burning across the city. Firefighters and physicians from across Nova Scotia, Canada, and New England descended to offer immediate help, while relief committees were established to aid survivors, 6,000 of whom were left homeless.

The toll of the blast was staggering. Fifteen hundred people were killed instantly, hundreds more died in the aftermath, and an additional 9,000 were injured. In all, 1,630 buildings were destroyed and 12,000 damaged. It is estimated that in today's money, the Halifax Explosion would have cost $430 million.

houses. With the advent of school busses in the 1950s, however, one-room schools were replaced with larger consolidated institutions.

- Number of children enrolled in Nova Scotia public schools in 1900: 98,000
- In 1950: 135,000
- In 2006: 138, 661

Take 5 WELDON RODENHISER'S FAVOURITE MEMORIES
OF GROWING UP IN NOVA SCOTIA

Weldon Rodenhiser, 69, grew up on Tancook Island off of Chester in Mahone Bay. He currently lives in Dartmouth with his wife, however, his mother still lives on Tancook in the summer.

1. One winter the water in Mahone Bay between Tancook and Chester froze. It took the ferry three hours to get across.
2. "You don't have storms now the way you used to," he says. Weldon remembers digging tunnels through the snow that he could stand up straight in. Back then there were no plows and everything needed to be shoveled by hand. Of course, he points out, there weren't any cars on the island either.
3. His father, a fisherman, would go sword fishing off of Louisbourg in order to pull in a decent salary of "four to five thousand dollars a year." His father could be gone for weeks and then one day just walk in the door.
4. Until the 1950s there was no electricity on the island and the family used oil lamps and a well. In the winter Weldon remembers breaking the ice in the well in order to collect the water in his bucket.
5. Weldon attended school in a one-room schoolhouse with a single teacher. Although he went to school straight through to grade 11, he and the other eleven kids from the island all failed the provincial exam that year because it was so hard. "Some professors in Prince Edward Island wrote it on a lark and didn't pass," he remembers.

FISHING

The fishery, like farming, has declined as a Nova Scotia employer. This is largely due to reductions in fish stocks, especially cod, a consequence of over-fishing. It is estimated that since the 1850s heyday of the Nova Scotia fishery, the number of cod living on the Scotia Shelf has plummeted by 96 percent.

Number of Nova Scotians engaged in fishing as their primary occupation in 1880: 29,976
- In 1901: 23,974
- In 1951: 15,607
- Today: Approximately 7,000 [Update to latest data available] Waiting on Call back from Fisheries department

GETTING AROUND

Just a century ago, horse and carriage, trains and boats were the main means by which Nova Scotians travelled their province. The introduction of the automobile, like it did elsewhere, changed forever the way Nova Scotians travelled and how they viewed their home province.
- Date on which the "horseless carriage" made its debut in Nova Scotia: September 11, 1899
- Year in which the first car was sold: 1904
- Cost per liter of filling up a car in 1904: 10.3 cents
- Year in which the first motor vehicle law came into effect: 1907
- Cost to register a vehicle in 1907: $5
- Cars registered in 1907: 62
- Number of cars in Nova Scotia in 1916: 3,050
- In 1956: 157,544

Did you know...

that in the 1920s and 1930s Nova Scotia was the world's largest producer of apples, but with the onset of World War II, the province lost its European market?

• Year that Nova Scotians began driving on the left side of the road: 1923

Today, of course, cars are ubiquitous in Nova Scotia. There are 586, 937 cars, motorcycles and busses registered in the province. These travel the more than 23,000 km of road and across 4,100 bridges managed by the Department of Transportation and Public Works.

Source: Department of Transportation and Public Works

ELECTRICITY

Life for Nova Scotians was revolutionized in 1884 when electricity was first introduced to Nova Scotians. The first to benefit were Haligonians, when 75 streetlights and 50 stores "went electric."
• In 1896, electric street cars were introduced to the province
• In 1919, the provincial Nova Scotia Power Commission was created

THEN COMES MARRIAGE

In Nova Scotia, weddings were traditionally community celebrations, planned for months. Community women worked together making quilts, linens and rugs for the couple and the wedding cake (a fruit cake) was made months in advance in order to properly "age" for the big day. The bride in a white gown, and groom in his best suit, were sometimes married in a church, but just as often at home in the family parlour.

After a honeymoon, the couple were welcomed home with a shivaree. Crowds would gather outside the newlyweds' home, making as much noise as possible until they were invited in for tea and cake. Today, marriages continue to be celebrated by friends and family, but with some modern twists. Hosting a wedding can cost the modern couple tens of thousands of dollars; the marriage license alone costs $100 while a courthouse wedding will run a new couple $75 plus tax.

Did you know...

that in 1901, Nova Scotia became the first province in Canada to manufacture cars?

Lunenburg

Old Town Lunenburg was added to the United Nations Educational, Scientific and Cultural Organization World Heritage List in 1995. It is only the second urban community in Continental North America to be included on this list. (The other is old Quebec City.)

Lunenburg received its designation because the Old Town is an outstanding example of British colonial settlement in North America, both in terms of its conception as a model town plan and for its remarkable level of conservation. Thankfully, Lunenburgers were just too practical to tear down buildings that were in perfectly good shape and replace them with the latest designs.

The town still adheres closely to the grid laid down by colonial planners in the 1750s, and more than half of the buildings downtown date back to the 19th century. Lunenburg homes have a widow's walk on the roof, a feature found in many seaports along the East Coast. The most peculiar feature of homes in Lunenburg, and for that matter Lunenburg County, is what is called the "Lunenburg Bump."

The "Bump" is essentially a four or five-sided dormer that over-hangs the front (and sometimes back) of the house. They are delightfully diverse, almost as if there was a competition and no neighbour wanted to be accused of imitation.

If you visit Lunenburg, don't confine yourself to just homes and the waterfront. The town has other architectural gems. The Lunenburg Academy (still a working school) is mistaken by many vis-iting children as a castle, and at night, lit as it often is by lights and the moon, you can understand why.

Although a 2001 fire claimed much of the two-and-a-half-century-old St. John's Anglican Church, it has now been completely rebuilt, standing again as the spiritual and architectural anchor of the town. St. John's is Canada's second oldest Protestant church and is one of the country's most outstanding examples of the Carpenter Gothic architectural style, the most dominant feature of which is that instead of rendering traditional elements of the church in stone, they are interpreted in wood.

HOUSEHOLD SIZE IN NOVA SCOTIA

1 Person	2 Person	3 Person
1991: 67,115	1991: 101,415	1991: 63,440
2006: 99,990	2006: 138,885	2006: 62,645

Expulsion of the Acadians

The first French settlers arrived in Acadia, an area consisting of present-day Nova Scotia, New Brunswick, and a part of Québec and Maine, in 1604. By the turn of the next century, there were upwards of 1,500 Acadians, a figure that would jump to almost 15,000 fifty years later.

Although it was the wars in Europe that caused Acadia to pass back and forth between the English and French during the 17th and 18th centuries, the battle in North America was also about numbers. Until the founding of Halifax in 1749, and the subsequent push on the part of the English to promote immigration, the Acadian population outnumbered the English-sponsored immigrants, something of which the colonial government took strong notice.

In 1713, a part of Acadia became Nova Scotia. Rather than leave, the Acadians chose to live under British rule. Asked to take an oath of allegiance to the British Crown, Acadians instead said they would remain neutral or sign a conditional oath stating that as long as they were not forced to take up arms against France, they would remain loyal to the British. Although there is some debate among historians, Gov. Richard Phillips is said to have accepted the Acadians' conditional allegiance in 1730, but simply forgot or failed to inform authorities.

In 1755, in response to French authorities building Fort Beauséjour on the present-day Nova Scotia/New Brunswick border, the English again raised this issue of the refusal by

4-5 Person	6 + Person
1991: 83,935	1991: 10,220
2006: 68,950	2006: 6,365

Source: Department of Finance

Acadians to swear their unconditional loyalty to England. This time, however, England began what is the most traumatic chapter in Acadian history. They claimed the entire Acadian population as prisoners, and from Beauséjour to Grand Pré, they loaded the Acadians onto boats destined for the colonies around the world.

From 1755 to 1762, it is estimated that three-quarters of the 13,000-strong Acadian population was deported; others fled, establishing remote Acadian communities that existed quietly on the fringes of society. Those who were deported were not only stripped of the land that they had spent a century or more cultivating, but they were only allowed to take the most basic of their possessions with them. In their wake, their villages were burned to the ground.

When Henry Wadsworth Longfellow's epic poem *Evangeline* was published in the United States in 1847, the story of the deportation and Le Grand Dérangement ("The Great Uprooting") was told to the English-speaking world. It was an immediate sensation and now has been translated into more than 130 languages. What *Evangeline* did was rescue the Acadians from being just a footnote in the history of the, New World, to being resilient people with a proud and enduring culture of their own.

In 2004, Acadians gathered in the province for the Congrès mondial acadien, a celebration of the 400th anniversary of the arrival of the first French speaking settlers in Canada. In 2005, Acadians commemorated the 250th anniversary of the deportation.

GAELIC

At the turn of the twentieth century there were an estimated 100,000 Nova Scotians who spoke Gaelic. After a century of forced assimilation and the growth of mass communication, Gaelic has nearly became a lost language; today just 500 Nova Scotians speak it. There has been a resurgence, however, due in large part to Gaelic language programs offered at Cape Breton's Gaelic College of Celtic Arts and Crafts.

The Bluenose

In 1920, The *Halifax Herald* newspaper sponsored the International Fishing Series, a race between working sailing ships. In the inaugural running, Nova Scotia was defeated and a New England vessel sailed home with the prize. In response to this disappointment, Nova Scotians hired a Halifax designer to build a Nova Scotian ship to contend for the prize.

The result was the schooner, the Bluenose, built in Lunenburg by Smith and Rhuland and launched on March 26, 1921. Captained by Lunenburg native Angus Walters, the Bluenose won every race in the International Fishing series from 1921 until 1938.

In 1929, the schooner was featured on the 50-cent stamp. In 1933, it represented the Maritime Provinces at the World's Fair in Chicago, and in 1935 the vessel attended the Silver Jubilee of King George V. Two years later, the image of the Bluenose was added to the dime. World War II, however, forever changed the sailing world, as wooden ships were being replaced with steel hulled vessels.

The 1938 sailing of the International Fishing Series would be the last. When the series was discontinued, Captain Walters fought to save the schooner, buying it himself to prevent its sale at auction. Four years later, however, she was sold to the West Indies Trading Company as a freighter. In January 1946, the Bluenose struck a reef off Haiti and sank.

SHAG HARBOUR

On October 4, 1967, several witnesses saw a bright, low flying object crash into the ocean in Shag Harbour off the southeast tip of the province. The object, still lit, bobbed in the water for about 15 minutes before sinking into the water. A final report from the Rescue Coordination Centre revealed that after 3 days of searching, no trace of the object could be found.

The origins of the object have been widely speculated. Some believe it was some sort of Russian vehicle, meant to spy on the then top-secret submarine detection base in Shelbourne. This story has been corroborated by one of the navy divers involved in the search, and the presence of both Canadian and US military vessels congregating in the area. Still others, such as one American naval diver claim that debris was found by the military, and that it was not from this planet. To this day, the Shag Harbour Incident (as it is often called) is considered by some to be the most significant UFO sighting in Canada.

Weblinks

The Nova Scotia Museum
— Heritage Attractions across Nova Scotia

www.musuem.gov.ns.ca

A website comprised of 25 museums across the province; historic buildings, living history sites, vessels and specialized museums.

Fortress of Louisbourg National Historic Park

www.louisbourg.ca/fort/

The Fortress of Louisbourg National Historic Site is the crown jewel of the Canadian Park Service and the largest historical reconstruction in Canada.

Not Black and White

THE SLAVERY FACT
Until 1833, Nova Scotia, like much of North America, was a slave-owning society. Many of the first black settlers in Nova Scotia were slaves and the relationship between black and white Nova Scotians was determined by this fact. Black people were widely held to be second-class citizens, and as non-citizens when they were the property of whites.

SLAVES AT LOUISBOURG
Between 1713 and 1758, at least 266 slaves lived on Cape Breton Island (then known as Ile Royale). Most lived at Louisbourg where they were domestic servants in French households.

THE "PECULIAR INSTITUTION" IN EARLY HALIFAX
The French did not have a monopoly on slave holding. Early English Halifax also accepted slavery as part of life. In 1751, a schooner named Success landed at Halifax, bringing "nine negro men" from Antigua. In 1752, a Halifax merchant offered to sell one female and five male slaves. The woman was described as ". . . a very likely Negro Wench, of about thirty five years of Age . . . and (was) capable of doing all sorts of Work belonging thereto, as Needlework of all sorts and in the best manner, also Washing, Ironing, Cookery and every other thing that can be expected from such a slave."

SLAVE OWNERS

On July 29, 1779, a Planter, Matthew Arnold, recorded that he sold "one Negro boy named Abraham now about 12 years of age, who was born of my Negro slave in my house in Maryland, for and in consideration of fifty pounds currency." For all their idealism about freedom, slavery still had a place in the Planter world.

Twenty Dollars Reward

Halifax Weekly Chronicle, 15 March 1794:
Twenty Dollars Reward

Ran away, on Thursday evening, the 18th inst a Negro Man Servant, the property of the Subscriber, named BELFAST; but who commonly goes by the name of BILL . . . At the time of the elopement he was in the service of William Forsyth, Esq.; and had meditated an attempt to get on board a ship that night which lay in the harbour, bound to Newfoundland; but was frustrated: It is probable, however, he may still endeavour to escape that way, therefore, the masters of all coasters going along shore, or other vessels bound to sea, are hereby forewarned from carrying him off at their peril, as they will be prosecuted, if discovered, with the utmost rigour of the law.

The above reward will be paid to any person or persons who shall apprehend and secure him, so that I may recover him again. He is a likely, stout-made fellow, of five feet eight or nine inches high, and about 27 years of age; of a mild good countenance and features, smooth black skin, with very white teeth; is a native of South Carolina, speaks good English, and very softly, and has been in this Province ten years.

When he went off, he wore an old Bath-Coating short coat, of a light colour, wore out at the elbows; brown cloth or duffil trowsers, also much wore at the knees; a round hat, and an old black silk handkerchief about his neck:— But as he had other cloaths secreted in town, he may have changed his whole apparel.

He will no doubt endeavour to pass for a free man, and possibly by some other name – **MICHAEL WALLACE**

Did you know...

that in 1832, the Cornwallis Street Baptist Church - the first African Baptist church in Nova Scotia - was founded in Halifax by Rev. Richard Preston?

BLACK LOYALISTS

One of the first groups of blacks to settle Nova Scotia were from the Thirteen American Colonies and loyal to the Crown during the American Revolution.

- 3,500 blacks living in the Thirteen Colonies came to Nova Scotia to join the 500 blacks, both slave and free, who already called the colony home.
- Black Loyalists were enticed by loyalty as well as promises of land and freedom.
- Black Loyalists found Nova Scotia's promises of land and of equal rights to be hollow.

Each family head had been promised 100 acres of free land, plus fifty acres for each person in the household. Black military officers were to receive 1,000 acres and privates, 100 acres. Such allotments never materialized.

- Only one third of black Loyalists received any land at all.
- On average, black Loyalists received fewer than 12 acres of land.
- Lands granted to black Loyalists were the infertile, often rocky tracts unwanted by white Loyalists.
- Black Loyalists found themselves competing with whites for work, and thanks to prejudice, often lost out in this competition.

Did you know...

that it was only in 1833 that the British Parliament passed the Imperial Act, which abolished slavery in the whole British Empire, including Nova Scotia?

RACIAL TENSIONS IN SHELBURNE

More than 1,500 black Loyalists settled at Shelburne, Nova Scotia, a town that was, in the late 18th century, experiencing unemployment and underemployment. Tense race relations existed in Shelburne from the outset. White Loyalists sought to drive black Loyalists out of town, mainly because black Loyalists worked for lower wages, undercutting white employment opportunities.

Tensions reached fever pitch when a black Baptist minister, David George, began to baptize whites. Although authorities did not disallow George's sacraments, George became the target of racially motivated attacks. A mob of hundreds of whites gathered, tearing down George's home, as well as those of his followers. Black residents of Shelburne were beaten and driven from town.

Fleeing black Loyalists re-established themselves at nearby

Bio MARY POSTELL

Mary Postell, a slave and daughter of a rebel officer, sought refuge with the British during the American Revolution and was granted her Certificate of Freedom. The document, however, would later be stolen and Postell would pay an enormous price.

After the war, and unable to prove her freedom, Postell moved to Florida where she found she was sold and resold by several 'owners.' When her master, Jesse Gray, moved to Nova Scotia, he took Postell with him. Fearing she would be sold again, Postell and her two children escaped Gray. She was found in Birchtown, however, and went on trial for her freedom.

At Postell's trial, two free blacks from Birchtown testified as witnesses on her behalf. For doing this, their homes were torched, and one of their children killed. Although Jesse Gray had misplaced his bill of sale for Postell, the courts sided with him and she was returned to him as his rightful 'property.' To punish his errant slave, Gray sold Postell for 100 bushels of potatoes.

They Said It

"Tolerance means nothing if it doesn't mean the acceptance of difference and therefore the preservation and maintenance of difference."
— George Elliott Clarke

Birchtown, leaving behind their homes and belongings. No aid was offered to the relocated blacks.

NOVA SCOTIA BORN

The percentage of the Halifax population that is African Canadian is four percent, the third highest proportion of any city in the country, behind Toronto and Montreal, according to the latest census.

- Chance that an African Canadian living in Halifax is third generation Nova Scotian or beyond, according to Canadian Social Trends: 8 in 10
- Chance that an African Canadian living elsewhere in Canada's cities is a third generation Canadian or beyond: 1 in 10

SEARCH FOR THE PROMISED LAND CONTINUES:

Sierra Leone

Black Loyalists did not find their hopes realized in Nova Scotia. Discrimination and poverty became their lot. A number of black Loyalists considered other options. Led by David George, a group of Loyalists accepted an invitation made by the Sierra Leone Company, a philanthropic organization that invited Nova Scotia blacks to relocate to the African Country of Sierra Leone. In January 1792, 15 ships containing 1,200 black Loyalists - about a third of all the blacks living in Nova Scotia - sailed to Sierra Leone.

Did you know...

that in 1890, Halifax-born George Dixon won the World Bantam weight boxing title, becoming the first black ever to win a boxing title?

Maroons

Another group of black Nova Scotians, the Maroons, originated in the British colony of Jamaica. For 140 years, beginning in 1655, Maroons fought their British colonizers. In 1796, they were subdued by the Jamaican government and the British deported the independent-minded Maroons. Five hundred and forty-three Maroon men, women and children were shipped to Halifax, where they landed in July 1796. Like the black Loyalists, the Maroons had high hopes for the freedoms they would enjoy in Nova Scotia; like the Loyalists, they were quickly disillusioned. After two hard winters, many Maroons followed black Loyalists to Sierra Leone.

Refugees of War

A third wave of black settlement in Nova Scotia coincided with the War of 1812. During the conflict, blacks in the United States sought the protection of the British. Two to three thousand refugees were brought by ship to Halifax in 1815. Most of these settled around Preston and Hammonds Plains.

Did you know...

that even today, African Nova Scotians feel the sting of racism? In a 2003 survey, 23 percent of African Nova Scotian parents said their children had experienced racial discrimination at school.

THE BAPTIST CONNECTION

Early black settlers in Nova Scotia found themselves excluded from the official Anglican churches of the colony. As a result, distinct black religious traditions emerged. Some of the earliest black settlers in Nova Scotia were well-respected clergy and would later be ordained by the Baptist church. While some, such as Shelburne's David George, ministered to black and white alike, perhaps the greatest legacy of Baptist clergy was the community and fellowship their congregations inspired. Baptist churches became important sites of cultural, social and political activities in black communities.

UNDERGROUND RAILROAD

People living in the communities of Preston, Upper Hammonds Plains, Guysborough, Lincolnville, Tracadie, Milford Haven and Boylston can trace their roots to the escaped slaves of the 19th century Underground Railroad. Traveling by night, relying on the constellations for direction, the runaways made their way from the American South through waterways, swamps, forests, mountains and back roads to the free northern states and to Canada.

With the assistance of such groups as the Quakers, free blacks and Native Americans, these bonded men, women and children were able to gain their freedom. At least 20,000 slaves escaped to Canada via the Underground Railroad, most of them crossing the border in Southern Ontario. Some of these refugees then made their way to Nova Scotia.

Did you know...

that in 1984 in Annapolis Royal, Daurene Lewis was the first black woman elected mayor in Canadian history?

Did you know...

that in 1993, Wayne Adams was the first black member elected to the provincial legislature?

AFRICVILLE

The story of the Africville relocation is one of the most heartbreaking in Canadian history. Africville, also known as Seaview, was a thriving black community on the outskirts of Halifax, on the Bedford Basin. It was settled by former slaves after the War of 1812.

Over time, the community grew to be a slum, in part a result of neglect heaped upon it by the city of Halifax. Africville was denied such basic city services as paved roads, street lights, running water, sewage and electricity. As the city expanded, Africville became the preferred site for such undesirable operations and facilities as a prison, a slaughterhouse, and a sewage dumping station. Although Africville was seen as a community of the destitute and downtrodden, the social cohesion amongst its residents was strong.

In the 1960s, Halifax City Council began to consider relocating residents, an option made all the more attractive by the vast business potential of the site. Proposed urban development plans included the construction of the A. Murray McKay Bridge and its related highway interchange system, and the Port of Halifax development at Fairview Cove.

In 1967, the city evicted the residents of Africville. Without deeds to prove their ownership of the land on which they had lived for 150 years, residents could not fight the city's plans. Paid $500 for their troubles, families were forced to leave their community and settle in poorly constructed public housing developments in Uniacke Square, Mulgrave Park and Spryfield.

Did you know...

that in 2002, Africville was named a National Historic Site? Unveiling the site marker, Heritage Minister Sheila Copps said of the Africville debacle, "the fabric has been torn apart, so the fabric can be mended. And what we're doing today is the beginning of a process that I hope will place the name of Africville on the lips of every Canadian."

THE IMPORTANCE OF PLACE: AFRICADIA

George Elliott Clarke coined the term Africadia to designate the land, history, and even the past and present existence of black Nova Scotians. Explaining this term, Clarke says, "I'm interested in rewriting the map of Nova Scotia. ...In the same way that the Mi'kmaq people have gone back to original Mi'kmaq names for many of the places in this province in order to lay claim to it, we need to reclaim the province because we have been disenfranchised; we've been ignored, we've been erased, in a sense, from the map."

CORRECTING HISTORY

In 2004, Nova Scotia's Black History week celebrated its twentieth birthday. The first such celebration was held in 1984, hosted by the Halifax North Memorial Public Library. In 1989, it became a month-long celebration.

KIRK JOHNSON: A BOXER FIGHTS THE SYSTEM

In April 1998, heavyweight boxer Kirk Johnson of North Preston was pulled over by five police cars, and his vehicle seized by an officer who claimed he did not have the correct papers for his car (he did). The next day, his car was returned, without apology.

Arguing that he had been the victim of racism and targeted as a result of racial profiling, Johnson brought his case before a Nova Scotia Human Rights tribunal. The boxer accused the Halifax police officers of pulling him over for "driving while black." The tribunal ruled that Johnson had indeed been a victim of racism. While the Chief of Police issued an apology, the head of the Police Association continued to deny that racism had been a factor. Johnson was awarded $10,000 in penalties.

Did you know...

that the United Nations has called on the Nova Scotia government to compensate the families displaced by the Africville relocation?

"IT'S TIME TO RECLAIM THE SCHOOL"

These words were spoken by Halifax Regional School superintendent Don Trider in the aftermath of an October 2, 1997 conflict between black and white students at Cole Harbour High School. On October 1st, a black and a white student engaged in a lunch hour fistfight. Later that afternoon, 40 students refused to attend class and hurled epithets at school staff. More than a dozen students were suspended.

The next day, the discord continued. When a fire alarm was pulled and the school evacuated, fights erupted in the schoolyard. As teachers and students alike feared for their safety, the school was immediately closed. With much trepidation, the school reopened, hoping that the weight of tighter security and discipline would prevent further fighting. Some observers, however, argue that until the century-old tensions between the student's hometowns, North Preston, a predominantly black community, and Eastern Passage, a white settlement, are improved, Cole Harbour High will be at risk for further violence.

They Said It

"The area is not suited for residences but properly developed is ideal for industrial purposes. There is water frontage for piers, the railway for sidings, a road to be developed leading directly downtown and in the other direction to the provincial highway."
– 1954 report by Halifax City Manager, explaining a reason for the relocation

"It's true I have a nicer home and I have hot and cold water and a bathroom but I haven't got happiness, that's one thing I haven't got . . . if Africville was built up again, I'd be the first to move back, I would."
– Former Africville resident

"There was just that sense of anywhere you go, anywhere you fall down, you hurt yourself, you don't have to go home, you go to the nearest house, then have that taken care of."
– Terry Dixon, former Africville resident

THE BLACK CULTURAL CENTRE

In 1972, Reverend Dr. William Pearly Oliver put forward a proposal to create a centre for cultural and educational programs to meet the needs and aspirations of the black communities of Nova Scotia. The Black Cultural Centre was the fruition of this proposal. Built on a three-acre lot just outside of Dartmouth, the centre opened its doors on September 17, 1983. It is operated by the Society for the Protection and Preservation of Black Culture in Nova Scotia (better know as the Black Cultural Society), which hosts a variety of cultural events across the province, including plays, concerts, workshops and lectures.

Weblinks

Black Cultural Centre for Nova Scotia

www.bccns.com

Historical information, upcoming events, music, heroes, and stories.

Black Settlement in Nova Scotia

www.museum.gov.ns.ca/arch/blkdata.htm

A virtual exhibit based upon the physical exhibit of the same title produced by the Nova Scotia Museum.

Black History Month Association

www.chebucto.ns.ca/heritage/BHMA/

A society dedicated to the development, contributions and achievements of African Nova Scotians.

They Said It

"If you pull one thing out to look at, then it seems quite simple, but when you begin to look below the surface you see how complicated that one issue is. And when you take several issues together, you have an intricate web that isn't easily pulled apart or fixed."

— **Parent of a Cole Harbour High student**

The First People

The Mi'kmaq are Nova Scotia's First People. Mi'kmaw territory, known as Mi'kma'ki, included mainland Nova Scotia and Cape Breton as well as New Brunswick, Prince Edward Island, the Gaspé Peninsula and Newfoundland. Traditionally, Mi'kmaw territory was divided into seven districts, each with its own distinct meaning:

Wunama'kik: "foggy land" — Cape Breton Island

Piwktuk: "where gaseous explosions erupt" — Pictou and P.E.I.

Eskikewa'kik: "skin dressers' territory" — Guysborough and Halifax counties

Sipekne'katik: "ground nut place" — Halifax, Lunenburg, Kings, Hants and Colchester Counties

Kespukwitk: "lands end" — Queens, Shelburne, Yarmouth, Digby and Annapolis Counties

Siknikt: "drainage place" — Cumberland County and the New Brunswick counties of Westmoreland, Albert, Kent, St. John, Kings and Queens

Kespek: "last land" — north of the Richibucto River and parts of Gaspé

- In 1860 the Mi'kmaq added an eighth district, Taqamkuk, southern Newfoundland.
- The word Mi'kmaq means "my friends." The Mi'kmaq originally identified themselves as L'nu'k, "the people." The word Mi'kmaw is the adjective form of Mi'kmaq.

THE MI'KMAQ TODAY

Today 24,175 registered indigenous people, most of them Mi'kmaq, live in Nova Scotia. Most live on 13 reserves, eight of which are on the mainland and five on Cape Breton Island. Approximately 4,000 Mi'kmaq live off-reserve.

About one in three Mi'kmaq speaks the Mi'kmaq language. In recent years, there has been a growing interest in preserving and revitalizing the language. In 1997, Mi'kmaq Online, a talking online dictionary, was launched featuring seven words and two sentences; today the site boasts more than 6,000 words as well as stories and songs.

LANGUAGE

The Mi'kmaw language, known by speakers as Mi'kmawi'simk, is a dialect of the Algonquian language stock, one of the two main Northeastern languages (the other is Iroquoian). It is related to other Native American languages like Ojibwe and Cree. Today the Mi'kmaw language has a written alphabet, but was traditionally conveyed orally

Did you know...

that there are several different Mi'kmaw dialects? Though all Mi'kmaq speakers can easily understand one another, the language spoken by Mi'kmaq in Cape Breton differs from that of New Brunswick.

or through pictographs. Contrary to popular belief, Mi'kmaw pictographs are not derived from Ancient Egyptian or Mayan hieroglyphs; they are North American in origin.

MI'KMAW PLACE NAMES AND THEIR MEANINGS

Antigonish: "where branches are torn off" [perhaps a reference to a location where bears would come to eat beechnuts or hazelnuts]

Chezzetcook: "flowing rapidly in many channels"

Eskasoni: "green boughs"

Joggins: "a place of fish weirs"

Kejimkujik (Lake): "attempting to escape," or it may also mean "swelled private parts," a reference to the physical toll of an eight km paddle across the lake

(Lake) Banook: "first lake in a chain"

Malagash: "place of games"

Merigomish: "a place of merry-making"

Musquodoboit: "suddenly widening out after a narrow entrance at its mouth"

Pictou: "an explosion"

Shubenacadie: "place where ground nuts occur"

Tancook (Island): "out to sea"

Tidnish: "paddle"

Tusket: "a great forked tidal river"

SUBSISTENCE

Before and after the arrival of Europeans, the Mi'kmaq used their land in a pattern of seasonal migrations and settlements. In the winter they moved inland where they lived in small family-based villages and

Did you know...

that the word "toboggan" comes from the Mi'kmaw word taba'gan?

hunted large game, such as moose and bear. For the bulk of the year, the Mi'kmaq relocated to larger villages at estuaries and on the coast where they relied more heavily upon the sea for sustenance. Although Mi'kmaq depended primarily on game, fish and foraged food (such as berries and wild plants), it is also possible that they grew crops.

Take 5 DANIEL PAUL'S
FIVE IMPORTANT NOVA SCOTIA MI'KMAQ

Born on the Indian Brook Reserve near Shubenacadie, Daniel Paul is a passionate Mi'kmaw historian, writer, and social commentator. In detailing a past that standard history books have chosen to ignore, he seeks to teach people of the damage that racism can do. His book, *We Were Not the Savages*, is a disturbing account of the genocidal tactics — including scalp bounties, starvation and germ warfare — used by British colonial officials in an attempt to exterminate and subjugate the Mi'kmaq. Paul was the founding executive director of the Confederacy of Mainland Micmacs, and is a member of the Order of Nova Scotia. When asked for his list of five most important Mi'kmaw leaders, he replied, "I have too much respect for the hundreds of individuals from our community who have made a difference for the Mi'kmaq to name five as my favourites. Therefore, I'll do five at random of the hundreds of my favourites."

1. **Chief Jean Baptiste Cope (Kopit), Shubenacadie Mi'kmaq District:** With the Treaty of 1752 and entering into a Friendship treaty with British Governor Peregrine Thomas Hopson, Chief Kopit laid the foundation for the modern day recognition of Mi'kmaw treaty rights by the Supreme Court of Canada.

2. **Former Pictou Landing Chief Raymond Francis:** Chief Francis, by determinedly opposing the use of Boat Harbour as an industrial waste lagoon, and resolutely seeking redress for the grievous

HOUSING

Traditionally, the Mi'kmaq lived in "wigwams," a word derived from the Mi'kmaw term wikuom. Women were responsible for building these conical watertight dwellings of birchbark, and could erect one in a single day. At their largest, wigwams could house 12 to 15 people.

wrong done to the band, single-handedly kept pushing until the band acquired legal counsel and sued its trustee. An out-of-court settlement is nearing $50 million, and a cleanup is in the works.

3. **Former Membertou Chief Ben Christmas:** In the late 1930s and early 1940s, senior Department of Indian Affairs bureaucrats decided that they would centralize the Mi'kmaq of Nova Scotia into two reserves. Chief Ben Christmas stands tall among those who fought diligently to end their disgraceful attempt to ethnically cleanse the Mi'kmaq.

4. **Sister Dorothy Moore, Mi'kmaw teacher:** Sister Moore is largely responsible for many of the positive inclusions of Mi'kmaw history and culture in Nova Scotia's school curriculum. She is a strong supporter of human rights for all peoples, and has fought diligently for equal opportunities for all.

5. **Elsie Basque, first licensed Mi'kmaq teacher in Nova Scotia:** Licensed in 1937, Elsie Basque successfully applied by mail to the Inverness County School Inspector for a teaching job at Mabou Ridge. When he met her, he advised that it would be best for her to go home because he felt that Mabou Ridge people would never accept a Mi'kmaq to teach their children. She refused to be intimidated and stayed.

HOW TO BUILD A WIGWAM

The frame of a wigwam consists of five spruce poles tied together at the top with split spruce root and spread out at the bottom to make a cone shape. Tie a hoop of moosewood around the poles, just down from the top, to brace them. Then tie shorter poles to the hoop to provide support for the cover of birchbark. Lay birchbark sheets over the poles like shingles, starting from the bottom and overlapping them. Extra poles can be laid over the outside to hold the sheets of birchbark down. Keep the top left of the roof open to allow smoke from a fireplace to escape. In bad weather a detachable piece of birchbark can cover this "chimney." Line the floor with fir twigs, woven mats and animal furs. A large hide (such as that of a moose) can be used as a door cover.

BIRCHBARK CANOE

This ingenious vessel allowed the Mi'kmaq to travel the tempestuous east coast of Mi'kma'ki, sometimes as far as Newfoundland. The first task in building an 18 to 24-foot canoe was to find a large birch tree that could provide the necessary bark. The frame or 'ribs' of the canoe was made of cedar slats. The ribs were then covered in sheets of birchbark sewn together with fir roots. Birchbark canoes were waterproofed using fir gum chewed by women and children. Canoes of the ocean-going Mi'kmaq had elevated gunwales to prevent waves from splashing into the craft and were propelled using beech paddles. After Europeans arrived, sails were also used.

Did you know...

that the word tipi was never used by the Mi'kmaq? It was a term used by another aboriginal group and refers to a dwelling made of skins, not birchbark.

SNOWSHOES

An innovative Mi'kmaw technology, snowshoes allowed the people to hunt and travel in Nova Scotia's deep winter snow. Men shaped strips of wood into oval waist-high frames, with curved ends tied together with moose leather. Centre supports were made using two slats of wood across the frame, about two hands apart. Women then took over the process and corded the frames in a crisscross fashion to support the toe, foot and heel.

Bio POET LAUREATE: RITA JOE

Rita Joe was born at Whycocomagh, Cape Breton in 1932 to Josie and Annie Bernard. As a young woman she met and married Frank Joe, and the couple moved to Eskasoni where they raised ten children. In 1973, Joe began her illustrious career as an author, writing stories and poems for the *Micmac News*.

By 1978, she had collected her poems into her first published collection, *Poems of Rita Joe*. Several more poetry and story collections, as well as an autobiography, followed. These solidified Joe's position as one of Canada's most accomplished writers. Her critically and popularly acclaimed writings have also earned her the unofficial title of poet laureate of the Mi'kmaw people. Her writing captures the beauty and complexity of Mi'kmaw culture — but more than that, it challenges the negative images that often stereotype aboriginal people.

Rita Joe explains her mission as a writer: "I want to put out positive images of aboriginal people. But everything I do is gentle persuasion. And that had more effect than a blockade or any other way — kindness, always. I teach my people to do the same."

Rita Joe and her work have been honoured with many awards. She has won the Nova Scotia Writers Federation Prize, received several honorary degrees, and in 1990, she was made a member of the Order of Canada. Rita Joe died in March 2007 at the age of 75.

MARRIAGE

Most commonly, marriage was a life-long union between couples. Before a wedding, the hopeful groom gave gifts to the bride's father to demonstrate his worthiness. If the union was approved, the couple was married in a days-long celebration that featured a feast provided by the groom, as well as games, singing and dancing. Weddings also provided an opportunity for the Mi'kmaq to recite their family trees — not uncommonly stretching back as far as ten generations! Although marriage was highly esteemed, the union could be ended by either spouse.

DIVISION OF LABOUR

Mi'kmaw men and women had different responsibilities based on gender, which were taught to children at a young age. Men hunted, made equipment (such bows, arrows, lances, snowshoe frames and canoes), and when it was required, engaged in warfare and diplomacy. Women were responsible for preparing food, gathering water and food, fishing and gathering shellfish and berries, tending children, transporting and skinning game, preparing hides and making clothing, crafting birchbark dishes, boxes and baskets, weaving mats, setting up wigwams, and transporting camp equipment.

GAMES

Games had an important place in Mi'kmaq society, as they cemented relationships between communities. The Mi'kmaq gambled, played a dice game, and enjoyed ball games using a ball made of caribou hide and stuffed with caribou fur. They also competed in bow-and-arrow contests and engaged in foot, canoe and swimming races.

MI'KMAW HEALING

The Mi'kmaq had the power to heal using their ingenuity, spiritual guidance, and knowledge of natural resources. They used emetics to induce vomiting, while swellings or boils were treated with blood-letting incisions. A favourite remedy for an open wound was the application of a piece of beaver kidney, which served to absorb blood and pus. The Mi'kmaw treatment for drowning was one that both alarmed and impressed early Europeans. The apparently lifeless victim would be administered a smoke enema, and then was hanged from a tree by the ankles until he revived. Early Europeans benefited much from Mi'kmaw medicine — the Mi'kmaw cure for scurvy, a tea made of alder, saved the lives of explorer Jacques Cartier and his crew in 1534.

SWEAT LODGE

Sweat lodges are important to Mi'kmaq spiritual and physical health. These lodges, a wigwam frame covered in birchbark and skins, featured a shallow pit that holds red-hot stones that have been heated in a fire. For an hour at a time, Mi'kmaq men sit around the pit, chanting, meditating and telling legends. At the end of this ritual, the men would run to a nearby lake or roll in the snow.

MI'KMAW HERBAL MEDICINES

(Don't try this at home! If used incorrectly, it may be poisonous.) The Mi'kmaq used a number of poultices and drinks to prevent illness and to heal and cure disease:

Ground Juniper
- **Ailment:** kidney ailments, especially bladder infections, diabetes.
- **Application:** Juniper twigs are cut off at the ends and boiled to make a drinkable tonic.

White Spruce Tree
- **Ailment:** colds, tuberculosis, laryngitis, mouth sores.
- **Application:** for lung ailments, a cup of tonic made of boiled branches and bark should be consumed at least twice a day. Sap can be scraped from the bark and applied to mouth sores.

Alder

- **Ailment:** rheumatism, stomach and kidney problems, fever, neuralgia and migraine headaches.
- **Application:** Soak shavings from the inner bark in water, along with a dash of peppermint. The shavings are then applied to the person's head, and held in place by a towel-wrap. The towel and the shavings should be replaced daily.

Cherry Tree

- **Ailment:** colds and flu.
- **Application:** boil the bark for an hour, then drink two cups of the tonic a day.

Flagroot

- **Ailment:** preventatively, for colds, coughs, flu, stomach ailments and colic in babies.
- **Application:** ingest the root of the plant. When combined with sarsaparilla, it makes a cough medicine.

Golden Thread

- **Ailment:** stomach ulcers, diarrhea, colds, influenza, diabetes, chapped lips, cuts and abrasions.
- **Application:** steep as a tea. For external use, it can be boiled with animal fat and once cooled, it is used as a salve.

Did you know...

that in 1992, history was made when Eleanor Johnson of Eskasoni wrote the first Masters thesis entirely in the Mi'kmaq language? Johnson's Mi'kmaq was written for the Anthropology Department at Saint Mary's University in Halifax.

MI'KMAW SPIRITUALITY

The Mi'kmaq believed the invisible, omnipresent and omnipotent Creator, the Great Spirit, created the universe. Like many aboriginal groups, they were animistic, seeing humans as part of a multilayered universe in which all animals and objects contain an identity and spiritual essence.

All animals and things have 'person' features, and people, animals and objects can change shape. The spiritual world and the physical environment are not separate, and they interact continuously. For example, the Mi'kmaq believed animals could reincarnate themselves from small segments of their bodies. This belief is what underlies the Mi'kmaw teaching that all parts of a killed animal must be respected and preserved.

A puoin is a highly respected person who communicates with the unseen spirit world. Aided by a medicine bag containing bones, pebbles, carvings and other sacred objects, puoins had important powers. They could locate game and fish, forecast the weather and predict the actions of spirit-beings.

THE SOUL

The Mi'kmaq believed humans were made of three elements: the body, the 'life soul' (the activity of the heart, lungs, circulation and motor functions) and the 'free soul,' which existed outside the physical form and was a shadow of the person. There were two varieties of free souls: those of the living and those of the dead. After death, the free soul travelled to the 'Land of the Souls,' but could return to earth to haunt the living. The Mi'kmaw afterlife was peaceful for all.

MI'KMAW FUNERALS

Death was not a prerequisite for a Mi'kmaw funeral. In some cases, a funeral would be held for the incurably ill, before they died. The dying individual would offer a farewell speech, which was followed by feasting and dancing.

Tobacco was important in funeral rites, as offering tobacco to the spirits aided the dead in getting to the spirit world. Dogs were often killed as a sign of grief and spouses mourned their dead husband or wife for a year. Every ten years or so, the Mi'kmaw dead were brought together and buried at a single site — an event that was also celebrated with feasts, dancing and speeches.

MI'KMAW CATHOLICISM

The Mi'kmaq were first exposed to Roman Catholicism when the French settled in Mi'kma'ki in the early 17th century. Their attitude towards this new religion was one of both curiosity and openness.

They allowed Jesuit priests to live and work among them, and in 1610, Grand Chief Membertou became the first Mi'kmaq to convert to Christianity. Remarkably, the Mi'kmaq accepted the spirituality of the Catholic Church without abandoning their own religious views; they saw Jesus as a natural brother to Klooscap.

The special relationship with the Catholic Church was formalized in a 1610 agreement between the Mi'kmaq and the Vatican known as the Mi'kmaq Concordat. With this treaty, which was spelled out on a wampum belt, the Mi'kmaq agreed to protect French settlers and priests in their territory and gave the Catholic Church access to Mi'kmaw lands for the purpose of building churches. In return, the Church recognized the Mi'kmaq as a Nation with its own inherent laws, customs, and religious authority.

This blending of the two traditions into one distinct faith remains strong today as Mi'kmaq Catholicism. The patron saint of the Mi'kmaq is St. Anne, the grandmother of Jesus Christ. On July 26th the Mi'kmaq celebrate 'the Grandmother' in St. Anne's Day celebrations across the province, and especially at Chapel Island, Cape Breton.

MYTHS

Myths and stories serve a very important purpose in Mi'kmaw culture. They are intended to teach children how things came to be and to explain the workings of the universe. They serve as a constant reminder to the people of their place in the complex universe.

KLUSCAP (GLOOSCAP)

One of the most important figures in Mi'kmaw mythology is Kluscap. Given his power by the Great Spirit, Kluscap was regarded as an important creator and teacher of the Mi'kmaw people. He created Mi'kma'ki and all its animals, giving them their shape and size. He also taught the Mi'kmaq to hunt, fish, cultivate and travel by the stars.

Kluscap lived in a wigwam at Cape Blomidon, which he shared with his family, an adopted grandmother and a young boy named Marten. From there, his hunting ground was far ranging and included Newfoundland, the Maritimes, Maine and Quebec's Gaspé Peninsula.

When Kluscap's work was done — when he had finished creating and teaching the Mi'kmaq people — he hosted a great feast for the Mi'kmaq at Blomidon. Then he left the people, stepping into his canoe made of stone, and paddled out to sea. As he left he told them that those who lived kind and just lives would live forever beside him. No one knows where he went, but he travelled up a peaceful river where he waits until the day he returns to the people.

Another home of Kluscap is Kelly's Mountain in Cape Breton, which is regarded as a sacred site in Mi'kmaw cosmology.

Did you know...

that October 1st is Treaty Day, an annual day to remember Anglo-Mi'kmaq treaties and their ongoing importance?

PETROGLYPHS

Petroglyphs are drawings etched in rock that are found around mainland Nova Scotia. They depict hunting and fishing scenes, Mi'kmaw myths and rituals, and supernatural figures. There are about 50,000 of these rock drawings at Kejimkujik National Park.

Sites have also been found on the Bedford Barrens and outside of Dartmouth. A prominent theme in Mi'kmaw rock art is the culloo, a long-necked, heron-like bird. Records from the 17th century show that the culloo was seen by the Mi'kmaq as playing an important role in transporting the soul to the other world.

POLITICAL STRUCTURE

There were three levels of leadership in Mi'kma'ki: local, district and regional. Each Mi'kmaw community was headed by a sagamore, or chief. Sagamores were selected according to a number of criteria: To a degree, leadership was hereditary, often being passed down the male lineage from father to son or nephew. But a leader also had to demonstrate his ability as a hunter or a warrior, and sagamores who did a poor job were not tolerated.

Sagamores did not rule dictatorially, but by persuasion. Generosity was highly valued in chiefs; as the best and cleverest hunter, a sagamore would provide food and furs for his people, and receive nothing in return. District and regional chiefs participated in the Mi'kmaq Grand Council.

They Said It

"The stated purpose of this exercise [centralization] was to make it easier for bureaucrats to administer our people at two central locations. But the effect was to take more of our people off the land, deny them their livelihood and force them to live on two overcrowded containment centers."
— **Alex Christmas, President of the Union of Nova Scotia Indians, Eskasoni, 1992**

THE GRAND COUNCIL

The Grand Council (Sante' Mawiomi) was the governing body that united Mi'kma'ki. It consisted of sagamores elected from each of the seven territorial districts, who in turn elected a kji'saqmaw, or Grand Chief, the ceremonial head of state. The other officers of the Grand Council were the Grand Captain (kji'keptan), who advised on political affairs, and a putus, who remembered the treaties and kept the constitution.

Several times a year, the Grand Council met to decide where families might hunt, fish and set up camp. They also dealt with relations with other First Nations. When the Mi'kmaq embraced Catholicism in the 17th century, St Anne's Day became an important meeting time of the Grand Council. Today, Grand Council representatives are community chiefs.

THE WABANAKI CONFEDERACY

The Mi'kmaq were also part of a larger political organization, the Wabanaki Confederacy. This was a loose coalition of five eastern Algonquian tribes who banded together to counter Iroquois aggression and collaborate on the bigger issues of diplomacy, war and trade. The other nations were the Maliseet, Passamaquoddy, Penobscot, and the Abenaki of present-day New Brunswick, Maine, New Hampshire and Vermont. Although the confederacy officially disbanded in 1862, the five tribes remain close allies today.

TREATIES

During the 18th century, as France and Britain vied for control of North America, the Mi'kmaq were important players in the conflict. No mere pawns in the imperial struggle, the Mi'kmaq sided with France and actively fought to drive the British out of their lands. Beginning in 1725, Mi'kmaq-British animosity began to subside when a "treaty of peace and friendship" was signed between the two nations. Subsequent treaties followed in 1728, 1749, 1752 and 1760.

The Mi'kmaq agreed to "bury the hatchet" and cease their attacks on the British. Although they did not surrender their sovereignty or land ownership, the Mi'kmaq agreed to allow the British to use their lands. In return, the British promised to protect Mi'kmaq territory and to allow the Mi'kmaq to continue hunting and fishing "unmolested."

In 1999, the Supreme Court's Marshall decision was a landmark recognition of these earlier treaty rights. It determined that the treaties signed between the Mi'kmaq and the British in 1760 give the Mi'kmaq a communal right to hunt, fish and gather in pursuit of a "moderate livelihood." A later court ruling would place limits on this right.

CENTRALIZATION

By the early 1900's, the Mi'kmaq were living on 40 small reserves scattered around Nova Scotia. Beginning in 1942, the Government of Canada embarked on a policy of centralization that saw the relocation of over 2,000 Nova Scotia Mi'kmaq onto two main reserves: Eskasoni in Cape Breton, and Shubenacadie on the mainland. Each of these reserves doubled in size as a result.

The government believed that this relocation would improve its ability to efficiently provide services to the Mi'kmaq. The plan, however, was disastrous for the natives. They were not consulted about the move, and many felt coerced to relocate, threatened with the prospect of losing federal services.

Many had given up good farmland to move to new locations that had poor soil. What the two communities also lacked was adequate housing and employment opportunities. The centralization policy was essentially abandoned by 1949. When the promised benefits of the new communities failed to materialize, many Mi'kmaq undertook the arduous task of re-establishing themselves in their former communities.

Weblinks

Mi'gmaq-Mi'kmaq Online
www.mikmaqonline.org/
The talking dictionary!

Native Council of Nova Scotia
www.ncns.ca
The self-governing authority for the large community of First Nations Peoples residing off-reserve in the province throughout traditional Mi'kmaq territory.

Mi'kmaq Portraits Collection
www.museum.gov.ns.ca/mikmaq/
The Nova Scotia Museum's Mi'kmaq Portraits Collection is a database of more than 700 portraits and illustrations that provide a glimpse into history.

Take Five

This chapter is designed to be fun, but at the same time revealing, both about our province, and the person making the choices. It is a chapter that could have continued well beyond the bounds of this book. Nova Scotians, famous and not so famous, were literally bursting at the seams with opinions about their province. This means, of course, we'll include more choices next time.

TAKE 5: ASHLEY MACISAAC'S FIVE FAVOURITE NOVA SCOTIANS

When Ashley MacIsaac burst onto the world music scene in 1995 with his debut CD, "Hi, How Are You Today?" he became an overnight pop icon — the kilted rebel from Creignish. MacIsaac has heeded well his father's advice: "If you want to play the fiddle, get mad at it or don't play it at all." His energetic genius has stretched that instrument far beyond the traditional jigs and reels, weaving in such contemporary styles as punk, electronica, hip-hop and grunge.

1. **Alexander Graham Bell:** I am fascinated with him for his inventions, particularly his work with the deaf and blind girl Helen Keller. He was an amazing Scotsman/Cape Bretoner.

2. **Allan J. MacEachen:** This Deputy Prime Minister — from Cape Breton as well — served under Pierre Elliot Trudeau. When Trudeau was out of the country, he could lay claim to Acting Prime Minister. He also was health minister during the implementation of Canada's health care system. He is one of my biggest heroes.

3. **Rita MacNeil:** Through all adversity, this artist has proven that the power of music is something that can supersede image, financial background and stereotypes, not only in the music industry but in our country and around the world.

4. **Jerome Sullivan:** My English teacher in high school. He proved that with the right instruction and an adherence to fine literature and art, even little kids living in the woods can come to appreciate the finer things the creative world has to offer.

5. **Hank Snow:** A man who performed thousands of shows and songs recorded by such greats as Elvis Presley, Anne Murray and countless others, proves that even a small town boy from Nova Scotia can make it to the biggest stages in the world of show business.

TAKE 5: NANCY STEVENS' FIVE FAVORITE LANDSCAPES

The Nova Scotia landscape has been an inspiration for painters for centuries. Noted among them is Nancy Stevens, a Fine Arts graduate of Mount Allison University who has taught landscape painting at NSCAD and St. F.X. University. Although her current interests are on large acrylic abstracts, Stevens continues to be drawn to the elements of shape and colour found in Nova Scotia's countryside and coastlines.

1. **Martinique Beach:** This location always provides inspiration: the pinks and purples of the rocks and the surprisingly turquoise water; at other times the division of space on the paper of a dramatic sky and sea or the textures of a foreground of pebbles and beach grasses.

2. **Annapolis Valley:** Several Annapolis Valley apple orchards have been my subject matter, especially in spring when in blossom and in late summer laden with ripe fruit. The regular pattern of trees, the rounded forms of distant hills and a meandering Avon river have wonderful design possibilities.

3. **Antigonish Harbour:** I always marvel at the ever-changing Antigonish Harbour, fields in foreground and forested hills on opposite shore. I have painted this landscape in winter when the harbour has been frozen, the land snow-covered, dark conifers patterning the whiteness; and in autumn when the colours were glowing and warm, the atmosphere soft and the water reflected a hazy light.

4. **Yarmouth County:** Painting the coast of Yarmouth County often presents a challenge because of the moisture in the air. When I painted the graceful arc of the beach at Port Maitland, the colours were muted and I tried to capture a quality of light that blurred the horizon and made the opalescent colours of wet and dry sand and shallow water dance and shimmer.

5. **Lake Ainslie:** Using both watercolours and acrylics to paint the hills surrounding Lake Ainslie, I have often been intimidated by the drama of that landscape. Vignettes of fields of goldenrod and late summer grasses sloping down to the lake accented by dark spruce, and a group of trees where eagles nest high on a hill overlooking the lake, have been more successful than the big scene.

TAKE 5: JOEL PLASKETT'S FIVE FAVOURITE HALIFAX HANG-OUTS

Joel Plaskett was only 14 when he formed Thrush Hermit, the alternative rock band that grew from its suburban Clayton Park roots into a modest success in the vibrant Halifax indie pop-grunge explosion of the 1990s. Now in his mid-thirties and playing both solo gigs and with his Joel Plaskett Emergency band, the lanky singer-songwriter-guitarist has over a dozen recordings under his belt. And despite a 2003 reader's poll in *The Coast* newspaper that voted him one of the 'Most Likely Haligonians to Move to Toronto,' Plaskett says he's staying put. He's even immortalized his hometown in "Love this Town," a homage to Halifax recorded on his CD, "LaDeDa" in 2005. Joel Plaskett Emergency followed up with "Ashtray Rock" in 2007 to rave reviews everywhere, scoring seven nods at the 2008 East Coast Music Awards.

1. **The Last Word Bookstore**, on Windsor Street in Halifax. "I like going here to talk about crime novels with the owner, Wayne."

2. **The Woodside Ferry Terminal parking lot**, towards Eastern Passage. "I like going here to eat take-out food while staring at the oil rigs."

3. **The Armview Restaurant** on Chebucto Rd at the rotary. "I like the rice pudding, the quiet, and watching cars go round in circles."

4. **Little Nashville**, on Wyse Road in Dartmouth. "This is like Nashville, only smaller."

5. **The Halifax-Dartmouth Ferry**. "Fifteen minutes to myself, and someone else is driving . . . a great way to start or end your day or night."

TAKE 5: ECOLOGY ACTION CENTER'S FIVE TOP ENVIRONMENTAL ACHIEVEMENTS

After almost 35 years in operation, Nova Scotia's Ecology Action Centre has a membership of more than 700, a volunteer force of over 200, seven active issues committees and a dozen or so people on staff. Over the years they have fought to protect endangered species, wilderness areas, deep sea corals and pedestrian-friendly cities. The staff at EAC have collectively come up with a list of what they consider to be Nova Scotia's top five environmental achievements:

1. **The Gully Marine Protection Area:** The Gully was the first Marine Protected Area in Atlantic Canada. It lies off the coast of Nova Scotia and is home to a vast number of marine species, from corals to whales.

2. **Nova Scotia's Wilderness Protection Act:** Since its enactment in 1998, the Wilderness Protection Act has secured over 33 protected areas, including the most recent acquisitions of Gully Lake and Eigg Mountain.

3. **Pesticide By-law:** HRM adopted Nova Scotia's first pesticide by-law and has since prevented the usage of gallons of harmful chemicals. Pesticide by-laws are now becoming major issues in other Nova Scotian municipalities.

4. **The Nova Scotia Recycling Program:** Starting in the early seventies as a group of volunteers collecting paper in Halifax, the Nova Scotia Recycling Program has grown province-wide and is now one of the best programs for recycling in North America.

5. **Support for local and organic foods:** The increasing successes of Nova Scotia's many farmer's markets is a strong indication of the mounting interest in buying local and environmentally-friendly foods. Farmer's markets are now all over Nova Scotia, including North America's longest running farmer's market in Halifax.

TAKE 5: TIM TREGUNNO'S FIVE HARDIEST NOVA SCOTIA FLOWERS

Tim Tregunno is the president and general manager of Halifax Seed. He is third generation owner of the oldest operating seed company in Canada (established in 1866). A lifelong resident of Nova Scotia (excluding a short stint during university days in New Brunswick), he has been involved in the business since 1979 on a full-time basis, and for many other years as summer employment.

1. **Lupin**
2. **Daylily**
3. **Petunia**
4. **Black-Eyed Susan**
5. **Shasta Daisy**

TAKE 5: HARV STEWART'S TOP FIVE SPORTING FIGURES

Harv Stewart has been sports director and a morning show co-host at Q-104 Radio since 1990. He is also the of host Eastlink's *Harv's Sportsland*. Prior to coming to Nova Scotia, he worked in Alberta covering the Oilers, Eskimos, Flames, Stamps and the 1988 Winter Games. He now calls Nova Scotia and Halifax his full-time home.

1. **Sidney Crosby:** At age 18, has dominated every hockey league he's played in and is now going to the NHL. He has the same characteristics — poise, humility and grit — of other greats like Howe, Gretzky and Lemieux. He is now being asked to help resurrect the NHL, a league that's been decimated by labour trouble. He is currently one of our most famous Canadians, and still a teenager!

2. **Colleen Jones:** Could be listed as the best curler ever, male or female. Her resumé of World and Canadian women's titles tells the story. She has only gotten better with age.

3. **Al MacInnis:** The pride of Port Hood — one of the best NHL defensemen ever to play the game. He has won the Stanley Cup in Calgary, the Norris Trophy, and an Olympic gold medal. He is the complete package. He came up as the hardest shooter in the league, but then refined his other skills to become a team leader and future Hall of Famer.

4. **Steve Konchalski:** Has been the head basketball coach at St. F.X. University for more than thirty years. He has led the X-Men to several national titles and was also the Canadian senior men's coach. His recruiting and teaching success are legendary.

5. **Don Koharski:** The Dartmouth native is the one you're not supposed to notice — the NHL official. But in the NHL, he is the man the league uses as referee in crucial games. He has appeared in more than ten Stanley Cup finals.

TAKE 5: TRUDY FONG'S FIVE FAVOURITE NOVA SCOTIA BACKROADS

Trudy Fong knows all about getting off the beaten track. Once, on a three-year journey around the world, she got herself sidetracked in Hong Kong and spent over a year working for the daily newspaper, *The Hong Kong Standard*. She did finally make her way back home to Nova Scotia, where she continues to write about travel, among other things, from her home in Dartmouth. Fong is the author of the popular *Insiders' Guide: Off the Beaten Path, Maritime Provinces*, which is now in its fifth edition.

1. **Antigonish to Jeddore along Highway 7:** The portion of the Marine Drive, which follows Route 7 from exit 32 outside Antigonish until you reach Jeddore, presents a time traveller's picture of the Atlantic Coast. You can make a complete family vacation out of a tiny bit of geography, enjoying along the way some excellent nature, including eagles' nests and a salmon ladder.

2. **Digby Neck, Long Island and Briar Island:** This whole area is really part of the Bay of Fundy's long trail of prehistoric lava that runs along the coastline. It's also a prime location for whale and dolphin sightings and many species of migratory birds.

3. The Cabot Trail, or Route 19, which skirts the northern perimeter of Cape Breton Highlands National Park: Of course that means you get to start in the heartland of Nova Scotia's most musical region, next enjoy the vibrant village of Cheticamp, and then drive through forests of 300-year-old sugar maples, yellow birch and beech trees. On a clear day you can see the Magdalene Islands.

4. Liverpool to Shelburne: From historic Liverpool south along Highway 103/Route 3 until Shelburne you can have a complete vacation in the palm of your hand. First you have the wilderness offered by the Kejimkujik Seaside Adjunct and Pocket Wilderness areas. Then you can follow Route 3 into the pretty village of Lockeport, site of the province's first officially designated heritage streetscape. Right alongside the entrance to the town is Crescent Beach, one of the province's finest, and as warm as you are going to get on the Atlantic Coastline.

5. Glooscap Trail: Skirting the shores of the Minas Basin any time of the year is a scenic delight. From Windsor, leave Highway 101 at Exit 5 and follow Route 215 along the Glooscap Trail. Here the world's highest tides reach their peak at Burntcoat Head.

TAKE 5: MARJORIE WILLISON'S FIVE FAVOURITE EDIBLE PLANTS

Since moving to Nova Scotia in the early 1970s, Marjorie Willison has thrown herself into the world of gardening. Today the popular columnist, author and phone-in guest applies that know-how to assist and encourage gardeners around the Maritimes to grow their own foods and flowers. Her books include *Easy Garden Planning* and *The Complete Gardener's Almanac: a month by month guide to gardening year round.*

Willison says it was easy to choose her five favourite plants — they are all edible.

1. **Indian Pear:** My favourite small tree has many names — Indian Pear, Juneberry, Shadblow, Serviceberry, and Amelanchier. I love its clouds of creamy white flowers in spring, and the rich, rust colour of its leaves in autumn. The dark summer berries add colour and flavour to fruit dishes of all kinds, and its multiple stems make a superb windbreak in winter.

2. **Raspberry:** The ubiquitous raspberry is my favourite cane fruit. Forest soil in Nova Scotia, exposed to sunlight after many years of shade, will produce raspberry plants from seeds long hidden in the soil. Just remember to cut out the old canes each year, and keep the clumps of canes thinned far enough apart that a dog could run through the patch.

3. **Potato:** Perhaps it is the Irish in me, but my favourite source of carbohydrates is the humble potato. Varieties developed in other parts of the world seem to thrive in Nova Scotia, perhaps because of our cool summers and damp soils. Whether you like them baked, boiled, mashed, scalloped, broiled, added to hodgepodge or turned into salad, potatoes nourish the body and comfort the soul.

4. **Tomato:** I can hardly wait each year for my first taste of garden-fresh tomatoes, my favourite annual vegetable. My favourite way of eating sliced, fresh tomatoes is covered with pieces of goat cheese, dressed with balsamic vinegar, olive oil, and a little salt, then garnished with snippets of fresh basil. Extra tomatoes are turned into a variety of soups and sauces, and also canned, frozen or dried.

5. **Asparagus:** My favourite perennial vegetable is marvelous asparagus, which comes up every spring in delectable spears without me having to plant it each year. A well-cared-for asparagus bed will produce for many years.

TAKE 5: COLLEEN JONES' FIVE FAVOURITE SPORTING ACTIVITIES

As a five-time winner of the Canadian Women's Curling Championship and two-time World Curling champ, Colleen Jones knows something about sports. Jones has been in the public eye since she won the first of 16 Nova Scotia curling titles for Halifax's Mayflower Curling Club when she was only 19 years old. Although she's considered the most successful Canadian women's skip in curling history, Jones doesn't confine her sporting activities to just curling. The woman who knows how to balance two careers and the demands of raising a family also knows how to enjoy her free time.

1. **Biking:** If you love to bike, the bike ride from Chester to Lunenburg on the old road (Highway 3) is fabulous—the hills aren't too painful. You start with a chocolate milkshake at the Windjammer for extra energy and you're set. It's been years since I've done the ride ... but the beauty is something that stays with you forever.

2. **Golfing:** I hate to golf, but I love to golf in Inverness at Highland Links. While my golf game is brutal, it's a fabulous walk with great views and apparently one of the best golf courses in Canada—which sort of goes over my head considering my game.

3. **Running:** While you'd have to travel many times around the world to find as great a running locale as Point Pleasant Park, I prefer the Frog Pond, on the Purcell's Cove Road. While I have yet to see one frog, you see plenty of ducks and the odd beaver building their dams. It's an easy run, with beautiful lake views on wooded paths ... a bit of paradise in the city.

4. **Rowing:** One of the oldest rowing clubs in North America is the Halifax Rowing Club on the Northwest Arm. I took lessons with my friend Linda Alexander—and while we had dreams of competing in

the Olympics, we had to settle for lots of Zen-like experiences at sixa.m. on flat water watching the sun rise over McNabb's Island.

5. **Swimming:** This one will always be heavily debated in the province, because some people love Liverpool, others Northumberland Strait, and others are Lawrencetown Beach bums . . . but for great sand, privacy and reasonably warm water, Bachman's Island in Mahone Bay is wonderful. Of course you need a boat to get there–a minor detail–but well worth the trip for swimming at your own private island!

TAKE 5: ALLAN LYNCH'S FIVE FAVOURITE PLACES

Allan Lynch is one of Nova Scotia's best and most prolific travel writers. His work has appeared in magazines and journals across North America and Europe. He brings with him wit and insight, the result of a lifetime spent traveling. As he puts it, trying to narrow down a list to five favourite places is tough because Nova Scotia is so deliciously diverse and eccentric.

1. **Annapolis Royal/Port Royal:** This is such a pretty, quiet area, it's hard to realize it's one of the most fought-over places in Canada. I also love the idea that this is home to the first permanent European settlement in Canada . . . that this is where the nation began. Few countries can claim to so definitively know their roots.

2. **Baddeck:** It's easy to understand why the beauty of this place so inspired Alexander Graham Bell. I also like the ability to cruise on the lake or visit the Gaelic College in nearby St. Ann's. One of the highlights for me is learning about Bell, the man, at the Alexander Graham Bell National Historic Site. His inventions are stunning, but the video memories of estate workers and his daughters are the real highlight of the museum.

3. **Lunenburg:** This is like some sort of fantastical architectural playground, with brightly coloured, overly decorated buildings. The streets are full of wonderfully pokey little shops and their calendar is stuffed with cool events from the Folk Art Festival, Folk Harbour Festival, and summer and Christmas crafts markets. The air also seems fresher here.

4. **The dykes behind Wolfville:** This is part of the legacy of the Acadians who were deported in 1755. Their ingenuity and back-breaking labour reclaimed thousands of acres from the sea. Four hundreds years later, the dykes are still doing their job, only now they provide a great place to walk and bike. In two minutes you can go from pavement to watching herons, harbour porpoise and seabirds.

5. **Our museums:** Nova Scotia is the pack-rat province. With more than 250 museums, we've shown our inability to throw anything away. The result is a truly fabulous collection of national historic sites as well as provincial and local museums.

TAKE 5: KELLY INGLIS' TOP FIVE NOVA SCOTIA DAY TRIPS

Kelly Inglis is the Marketing Director and part-time Editor at MacIntyre Purcell Publishing Inc. in Lunenburg. She currently resides in the charming community of Port Medway along the South Shore, and was more than happy to tell us her favourite day trips.

1. **Tubing:** I've experienced tubing on two rivers here in the province; the Gaspereau in Kings County and the Medway in Queens County. It's the most fun when you can get a group of friends together and spend the afternoon floating down a river on a hot day. Bring a roll of rope to link yourselves together and hang on when you hit the rapids!

2. **Upper Clements Park:** A theme park just outside Annapolis, it's a fun family outing complete with a rollercoaster, flume ride, bumper boats, mini golf, antique cars, live entertainment, and so much more. Directly across the road is the Upper Clements Wildlife Park, also a must-visit while there. If you have more than one day to spend in the area, a visit to Fort Anne (to see the huge hills) and the Habitation (to see the country's first fort replica) are definitely worth it.

3. **Bluenose Boat Tours:** Spend the afternoon aboard the Bluenose II for a tour on the water. See the beautiful waterfront town of Lunenburg from the best vantage point - upon one of the country's most loved schooners. Afterwards, a horse-drawn tour of the town followed by a great meal at one of the many restaurants will be the perfect cap to the day.

4. **Oaklawn Farm Zoo:** While driving through the Valley, make sure to make a stop at the Oaklawn Farm Zoo in Kings County. Exotic, native, and domestic animals all reside here at the province's largest zoo. The zoo is only a hop, skip, and a jump from the Bay of Fundy – the world's highest tides – so be sure to schedule a visit here as well.

5. **Cabot Trail:** This is a must-see, especially in the autumn. The majestic colours and scenery will truly take your breath away. Make a pit stop at the Fortress of Louisbourg along your way to send you spiraling back into time.

TAKE 5: ALAIN MEUSE'S FIVE FAVOURITE FISH STORIES

Alain Meuse has been editor of *The Sou'wester*, the commercial fishing newspaper of record in Canada for the Atlantic coast, for more than 30 years. From his perch in Yarmouth, he has witnessed the booms and the collapses of the most dangerous, volatile, and important industry in the province. He has also born witness to government double talk and tall tales, and he has relayed those to his readers for almost forty years.

1. **Bluefin Blue:** We were on a bus traveling back to Toronto from the RMC College in Kingston, Ontario, way back in the early 60s where our squad, the Ryerson Rams football team, had demolished the soon-to-be military geniuses 60 to nil when the talk turned to fishing. One fellow from Northern Ontario kept bragging about the three-foot northern pikes he caught the previous summer.

"Hey, Bluenose. What's the biggest fish you ever caught?" he queried moi.

"Well, not that many. Only went eeling when I was a kid. But I was on a boat once where an eight or nine incher was hauled in. Took the guy six and a half hours," I replied. Guffaws all around.

"Eight or nine inch? Eight or nine inch what, minnow?" he charged. More hee haws.

"Oh. Forgot to add that down east we measure 'em between the eyes, bys. The eyes."

Name was Bluefin Blue from then on . . . .

2. **Quiet Canadian:** It was early June and the water was low on the Barios when I decided to take my friend Hayden for some brook trout fishing. By that time fly fishing was the rigueur on that river but Hayden was and is a die-hard metal caster. They just weren't biting that day and to top it off Hayden kept losing lures to a weedy bottom and rocks festooned with green algae.

He looked a bit puzzled as he scratched around his lure box. He finally told me he was down to his last lure. I looked as he tied on a greenish bunch of fur and tassel on his line. Lord, I thought. Green thing-a-ma-jig with all that green stuff in the water? No chance in hell. But you don't correct a friend. Never.

I watched in amazement as on just his second cast he pulled in a pound-and-a-halfer. We left shortly after. After all, I was driving. Was a quiet ride back, as I remember. From my side anyway.

3. **Beaver:** My friend Bucky was fishing the Annis River one late sum-

mer evening when he tied into a monster 'salmon.' Try as he may he couldn't angle the thing close to the net. It came in, then stripped his line so hard and fast that his fly fishing reel began to complain. Now Bucky is a world class angler but even he couldn't figure out this one. And the night was closing in fast.

When the 'salmon' started to head out to the lake that empties into the river, Bucky knew the gig was up, in a way. Then a peculiar thing happened; his 'salmon' climbed onto a rock! He had hooked Canada's national symbol, the noble and ingenious beaver!

"It was a tough wade but I got my fly back anyway. He wasn't too pleased when I yanked the hook out of his fur but a good fly is a good fly," he said.

4. **Legend of Sneezy Mac:** I won't name the person to protect the guilty. He was trouting with a pair of friends one lazy summer afternoon. Well, they were fishing, he wasn't, tending a stash of cool Oland's Export Ale. But the boys couldn't land anything; hooked aplenty but nothing aboard the canoe.

"Give me the damn rod," he bellowed. One was handed to him. He took a piece of wool from his sleeveless shirt and some hair from his nostrils and asked one of the pair to tie his opus on the hook, which they obliged amidst giggles which almost tipped the canoe.

Lo and behold the fly worked like a charm. We named it Sneezy Mac on the spot.

5. **Let Their Be Light:** We were in camp one evening and over cards and 'coffee' the talk turned to big fish.

"Caught an eight pound brookie down by the Little Meadow last spring," a newcomer to the gang muttered. We all looked at him. No such thing as an eight pound brookie. Only in dreams.

"Well," drawled, one of the ole buddies. "Was jigging for cod out by Jacko last summer and what did I haul up but a ten pound cod with a hurricane lantern wrapped around his lips. And it was lit!" After the laughter subsided, the newcomer dared to question the fact of the lit lantern.

"Impossible!" he growled.

"OK," said the old buddy. "You take five pounds off your trout and I'll blow out the lantern!" Amen . . .

MICHAEL HAYNES' FIVE FAVOURITE HIKES

Michael Haynes has made a name for himself doing what he loves best: hiking the hills, highlands and coastlines of Nova Scotia. He has supplied Nova Scotian hikers with such guides as Hiking Trails of Nova Scotia, Hiking Trails of Cape Breton, and Trails of the Halifax Regional Municipality. Born in Nova Scotia, Haynes currently lives in Ottawa where he administers a national trails website (www.TrailsCanada.com) for Go for Green, a foundation that promotes active living in the outdoors.

All Haynes' picks share some common elements: They are all challenging hikes, either in distance or in ruggedness; each is located in an isolated corner of the province, and so tends not to attract too many visitors; and all of them except Franey follow the coastline. If you're a fairly experienced hiker and you like wild, authentic Nova Scotia nature at its best, we suggest you give one of these hikes a try.

1. **Polletts Cove, Inverness County**
2. **Franey, Cape Breton Highlands National Park**
3. **Cape Chignecto Trail, Cumberland County**
4. **Taylor Head Provincial Park, Halifax County**
5. **Gabarus to Belfry Gut, Cape Breton County**